SWINESEND

LOCKER, DORNAN & OWENS

ODI PROFANUM VULGUS ET ARCEO

SWINESEND

BRITAIN'S GREATEST
PUBLIC SCHOOL

Atlantic Books
London

First published in Great Britain in 2007 by Atlantic Books,
an imprint of Grove Atlantic Ltd.

9 8 7 6 5 4 3 2 1

A CIP catalogue record for this book is available from the British Library.

Illustrations by Dan Archer – www.archburger.com
Design by Five Twentyfive Ltd – www.five-twentyfive.com

ISBN   978 1 84354 520 0

Printed in Great Britain by
Clays Ltd, St Ives plc

Atlantic Books
An imprint of Grove Atlantic Ltd.
Ormond House
26–27 Boswell Street
London WC1N 3JZ

Why ~~Eton~~? Swinesend
~~Winchester~~
~~Stowe...~~

SWINES!
(formerly *The Swinesian*)

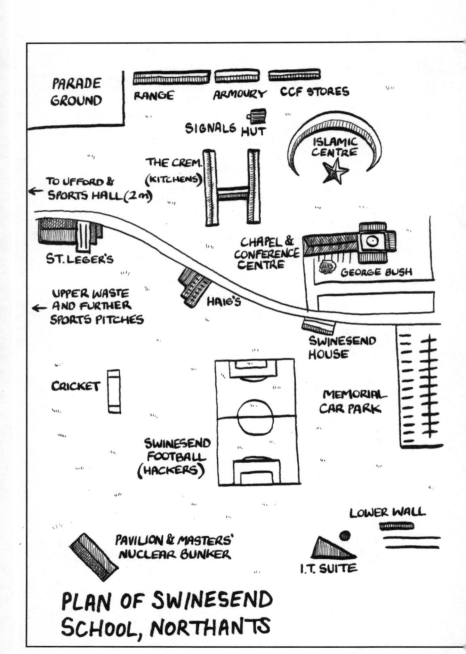

PLAN OF SWINESEND
SCHOOL, NORTHANTS

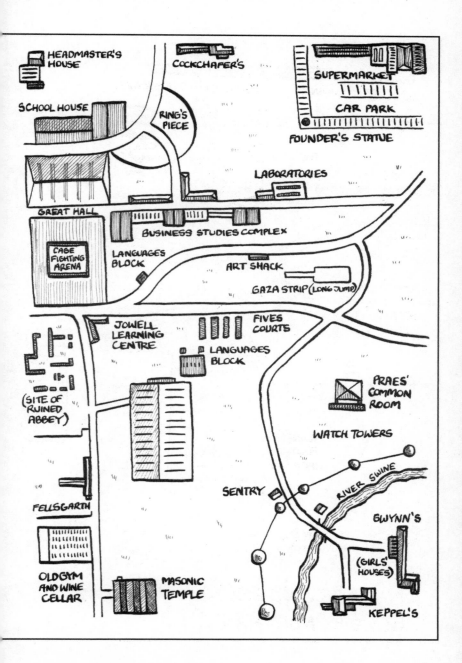

Why ~~Eton~~ ? *Swinesend*

Winchester

~~Stow~~...

LAST DAYS OF FREEDOM

ARE YOUR FRIENDS BEHAVING STRANGELY?

Only recently, your chums were helping you to pour petrol on the cat and drop bricks on passing trains, but they have now lost all relish for your latest pranks. Where once they sat on the few, fungus-spotted boards of the tree house and shared their knowledge of arcane swear words and imaginative names for the female pudenda, they are now in the grip of despair and hint darkly that you will soon be incarcerated in a bleak, icy institution dedicated to extreme boredom, incomprehensible rituals and unspeakable acts in the showers.

If this all sounds horribly familiar, there are two possible explanations for what is about to happen. To find out which one applies to you, sit down, take a deep breath and consult the chart overleaf.

Now that you have worked out what is to become of you, your first step must be to stop snivelling (if you have started). Your second is to to work out exactly where your parents are plotting to send you. You will probably have heard of establishments such as Eton and Harrow. Do not fall into the common trap of thinking that you will be sent to such places. Everyone else has heard of them too. Your parents will much prefer to patronize the people they want to impress by boasting that they didn't want to burden you with all the baggage that goes with attending those schools.

So, the chances are that you will be sent to a far better school, every bit as expensive and much better suited to your abilities. There you

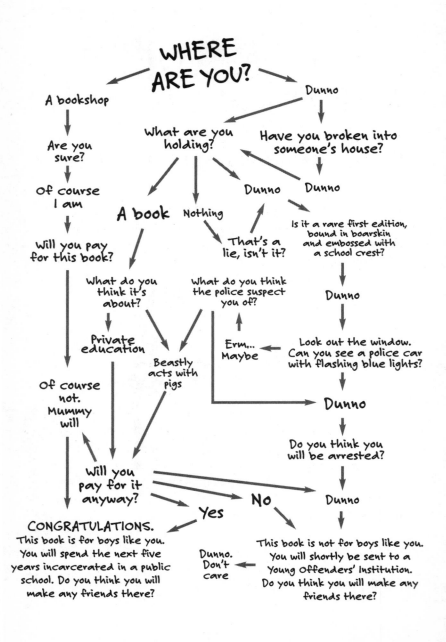

will be taught by strange men: curious individuals who will spend five years taking not the slightest interest in what you think and certainly not caring what you feel. There are many ancient establishments offering this wonderful preparation for future success, but the greatest one of all is Swinesend School.

THE TELL-TALE SIGNS

How can you tell whether you will be fortunate enough to be sent to Swinesend?

1. Your father starts living in the past

If your father attended Swinesend, it will have made him so bitter that he wants to inflict the same experience on you or, more likely, he won't have the imagination to send you anywhere else. The giveaway sign is a new tendency to harp on about 'The Good Old Place' and the way in which his experience with the rubber eel and a cheese-grater made him 'the man he is'.

If your father was not so fortunate but has made a good deal of money, he will remember the 'public school ponces' who used to look down on him when he started out. He will be consumed with a burning desire to show them that his money is as good as theirs and so will send you to the greatest school possible. He will almost certainly select Swinesend.

2. Your mother starts talking to herself

From motives of ill-informed snobbery, your mother may briefly consider other schools. Try and catch her when she's next looking in the mirror. If she thinks that she is unobserved, you might catch her practising a brand-new accent that will make her sound as classy and concerned as the Duchess of York confronted simultaneously by a West African amputee and a television camera. The phrase she will be repeating will tell you the name of the school she thinks will suit you best and, if you can consult the table opposite, you can easily work out why.

MOTHER'S PHRASE	TRANSLATION
Darling Robin is down for **Winchester**	My son is quite brilliant, unlike yours.
Darling Robin is down for **Eton**	My son is fairly bright, and will benefit from the opportunity to shove a future Prime Minister's head down the lavatory.
Darling Robin is down for **Harrow**	My son is not bright at all but our Mercedes will look good parked next to a Duke's second son's Range Rover on Founder's Day.
Darling Robin is down for **Shrewsbury**	I have no idea whether my son is clever or not, but Shrewsbury is every bit as good as Rugby, or Westminster or Charterhouse, whatever you might think.
Darling Robin is down for **Sedbergh**	My son might not be clever, but he is a fantastic prop and a pretty good hooker.
Darling Robin is down for **Stowe**	My son will not spend the next five years with the brightest boys but you should see the facilities we're paying for.
Darling Robin is down for **Swinesend**	At prep school, my son's Headmaster said this was the only school suited to my son's unique abilities. He also assured me that, now that the Press has forgotten about the incident involving the Under Master and the stuffed goat, Robin will certainly enter Britain's greatest public school.

3. Your parents start taking an interest in the neighbours

If your parents lived for years in peaceful ignorance of their neighbours, the Watsons, until the moment their eldest son (and your arch enemy) got a place at Radley, then you can be certain that your parents will be bombarded with invitations to summer drinks parties and evening games of whist – all so that your mother can listen to endless stories about how Simon made the Third VIII and how well he's doing in maths (all things considered). Then it can only be a matter of time before she realizes that there is only one unanswerable riposte which conveys all of her previous aspirations: that you are 'down for Swinesend'.

And once you've heard her say that, there's no way she'll lose face by sending you anywhere else.

4. You are encouraged to answer stupid questions

If these initial investigations leave you none the wiser, there is one final and foolproof way to work out where your parents plan to pack you off to school. You will start your final year at prep school sitting endless practice papers and, if you are destined for an ordinary public school, you will be made to sit the Common Entrance Examination. More exclusive institutions such as Winchester and Swinesend regard the Common Entrance as altogether too common and prefer to set their own test.

So, if you find yourself practising the following paper (which has remained unchanged since 1956) and are then dragged off one day to sit it, you can be certain that your parents' plans have come to fruition.

SWINESEND

ENTRANCE EXAMINATION

2007 ~~1999~~ HILARY TERM 1~~956~~ ~~89~~ 65 77

MATHEMATICS

1. If one Englishman is needed to rule 6,000 natives in 2,000 square miles of territory, how many Englishmen will be needed to rule the Sindh province (area: 54,407.585 mi²; population 4 million).

2. Schoolboy (a) has a pair of swimming trunks (b) and a swimming master (c) Under what conditions does a+c = a–b. (Answer breathlessly.)

HISTORY

1. What evidence is there that Vlad the Impaler invented the yo-yo? Illustrate his technique with diagrams.

2. If, as Erasmus argues, 'In the land of the blind, the one-eyed man is king' (*In regione caecorum rex est luscus*), what would happen in the event of a successful coup?

LATIN

Si hoc legere scis, nimis eruditionis habes.

FRENCH

Translate the following into French and quickly back again:
'It is unthinkable for a Frenchman to arrive at middle age without having syphilis and the Cross of the Legion of Honour.' (André Gide)

ECONOMICS

Assuming that 1,000,000 Irish died during the famine years of 1845–9, and 1,500,000 emigrated from a population of 8,000,000, how many more years of famine would have been needed to avert the Easter Rising of 1916?

SCIENCE (NON-SCHOLARSHIP CANDIDATES ONLY)

1. If friction generates both heat and censure, explain the best way to fix a bicycle lamp.

2. Prescribe suitable purgatives for three of the following maladies: spleen, hysteria, beastliness, melancholia, hyptertension, Crohn's Disease or Communism.

Some weeks after this examination, however, you will arrive home after a glorious spring day spent re-educating your best friend by duct-taping him to a local railway line, or teaching him the art of using cheese wire to bungee-jump from the town bridge. Fully content, you will nudge open the front door, only to be accosted in the hall by your mother, who for once will smile brilliantly, ignore the grime which you have wiped on the carpet, and appear delighted to see you.

She will point to a letter like this one, which she will have had framed and mounted on the wall, just next to the hat stand and in a position that no guest could miss.

It's official: from 10 September you will be a member of Britain's Greatest Public School.

Confronted with such news, the only thing you can reasonably do is react calmly. So, grab the copies of the prospectus and the School magazine which your mother has left prominently on a table in the hall, stamp up the stairs, jam your bedroom door shut with a chair and throw yourself on your bed. Then, when you feel stronger, pick up the prospectus. This is the publication with the cover that features photos of local people bowing their heads deferentially as two tail-coated youths stride past them in the town; a group of intellectual-looking Sixth Formers enjoying a glass of port whilst some even more intellectual-looking girls clear the remains of seed cake from the table; and two rugby players grinning broadly as they prise a smaller boy from the mud in which his mangled body has been embedded.

SWINESEND

The Headmaster and Chief Executive Office
Swinesend School
Nr Corby
Northamptonshire
18th June 2007

Mr and Mrs R.V.J Irvine
The Old Rectory,
Coldharbour
Surrey, GU7 6XP

Dear Mr and Mrs Irvine,

I am delighted that you have accepted the offer of a place for your son Robin
at Swinesend commencing next Michaelmas term. Robin scored 10 per cent
in the Entrance Examination and has been provisionally assigned
to St Leger's House.

I acknowledge receipt of your cheque for £2,000 payable to Swinecorp (Cayman)
(No. 2) Ltd. This is non-returnable.

I also recommend that you seriously consider investing in Swinesend Edubonds®
which provide many benefits such as school fees insurance, which will give you
peace of mind if you die in tragic and wholly unforeseen circumstances or there
is any accidental damage caused to Robin during his time at the School.
A sales person will be contacting you by telephone shortly.

I enclose a copy of our most recent school prospectus that I hope will answer all the
questions that Robin may have.

Finally, to remind you that term starts on 10 September next.

Yours truly,

Tim Taylor

Tim Taylor, CBE, B.Ed. (Loughborough)

Enclosed:
School Prospectus (including a short history of the School)
The latest issue of the School magazine (*Swines!*)

ODI PROFANUM VULGUS ET ARCEO

SWINESEND

BRITAIN'S GREATEST
PUBLIC SCHOOL
PROSPECTUS

Tim Taylor, CBE, B.Ed. (Loughborough) Headmaster

From the Headmaster

Congratulations on considering a most important investment in your son's future: the gift of a Swinesend education.

Just as Aristotle trained the young Alexander to be sound in mind, body and morals, our school prides itself on producing solid all-rounders who are well equipped to conquer the world. For every successful Oxbridge candidate we educate, we also turn out (on average) three damned good shots, a couple of officers in the Royal Engineers, twenty-five successful stockbrokers, two well-intentioned lawyers and one thoroughly decent chap.

Parents, envious headmasters, cabinet ministers and occasional heads of state often ask me: 'What is the secret of Swinesend's success?' To this question there is, of course, only one answer: The Future. We live in a complex and rapidly changing world and we prepare our boys by keeping them away from it as long as possible. Only with this training can they expect to make a wholly original and unexpected mark on Society.

During your son's time at Swinesend, we ensure that, in addition to a smattering of Latin and a healthy distaste for meritocracy acquired through academic study, he develops:
- the proper degree of difference from his inferiors;
- a powerful sense of his own abilities;
- a distaste for unpleasant displays of emotion, whether in private or public;
- an ambition to go one better than the next man; and
- a precise and detailed knowledge of what is, and what is *not*, amusing.

We realize, however, that only a visit to the School itself will truly take your breath away. If you would like to book a discounted tour of the School, please complete the form at the back of this prospectus and return it with the relevant payment to the Bursar.

If a personal tour is impossible, I trust that this brochure, complete with some of the findings from last year's report by the Independent Schools Inspectorate and details of follow-up visits by the NSPCC, the Health and Safety Executive, the Fraud Squad, the Office of Fair Trading, the Commission for Racial Equality and Special Branch will answer any further questions you may have about the School.

Tim Taylor, CBE, B.Ed. (Loughborough)
Headmaster

BUILDINGS

The School is proud to own the site with the highest concentration of demolished or de-listed Grade I and Grade II buildings in England: a record that has enabled us to build a memorial car park on the remains of the medieval Abbey that stood on Simpools Lane; add a conservatory to the masters' Common Room at the back of the Swinesend House (a Queen Anne building that was direly in need of modernization) and place a lightweight, aluminium storey on top of the twelfth-century chapel, enabling us to create a conference and banqueting suite that combines the splendour of a mock-Gothic environment with magnificent views of the School grounds and surrounding countryside.

These improvements, we believe, have enhanced the quality of pupils' experience and provided employment opportunities for local people. We are justly proud.

For other notable buildings, refer to the map of the School doodled by Simpkins as he was brandished upside down from an upper floor window for 16 hours, copies of which are now available from the Bursar's office for £45 (English version) or £75 (Latin translation).

INFORMATION SERVICES

The Jowell Learning Centre (formerly 'The Library') is also being refurbished and will from next term boast a fully equipped computer suite and special 'learning pods' (formerly 'desks'), sponsored by local businesses, at which pupils will be able pursue their own personal development goals. Legacy information formats (including 'books') will be kept in the rare manuscripts collection and will be available on request.

HOUSE SYSTEM

All pupils are assigned to a House, where they will live under the supervision of a Housemaster, two House tutors and a team of Praeposters (or prefects). Each house also has a matron. Boys are allocated to Houses which best suit their talents and characters.

Name of House	Housemaster	Preferred joining criteria
School House	The Headmaster	Sporting prowess or a larger than normal endowment.
Cockchafer's	Mr Reid	Early nights, kneeling and an interest in Scouting.
St Leger's	Dr Udall	Mathematical precocity and/or an interest in antiques. Immunity to female blandishments.
Haig's	Mr ffrench	Sacrifice and a refusal to accept failure.
Fellsgarth	Mr Napmann	Boys with an individualistic streak, railway hobbyists, dinosaur enthusiasts.
Gwynn's	Mrs Parker	Females.
Keppel's	Hon. Mrs Edgar Keppel	Richer females.

CURRICULUM

The curriculum is broad-ranging and designed so that pupils leave school fully able to contribute to the British and global economies. Traditional subjects such as Biblical Knowledge and Latin are still compulsory, but the School has also made a name for itself in subject areas as diverse as Entrepreneurship, Management Buyout Skills, Kangaroo Farming and Diversity Studies. Our track record in these areas means

that Old Swinesians who run businesses and quangos will be only too happy to help boys find an outlet for their talents when they leave school or university.

YEAR GROUPS AND PRIVILEGES

During their time at Swinesend, pupils progress through six forms. To encourage boys to develop a sense of personal responsibility, progression to a higher year group brings with it an increased number of privileges, which may be withdrawn at any time. Below is a list of year groups and the most notable privileges that membership of each confers.

Lower IV (formerly The Shell): No privileges.
Upper IV (formerly The Remove): Allowed use of shared study. May address college servants on Sundays.
Fifth Form: Permitted heating in shared studies for one hour each evening. May address college servants at all times. Allowed into town once a week. May walk across Ring's Piece arm-in-arm with another boy of the same age.
Lower VI: Allowed to address townspeople (if head is covered). Allowed to sit in centre of pews during Chapel. Allowed own studies, which may be heated for two hours each evening. Allowed into town during free periods.
Upper VI: May keep hands in pockets on Sunday and wear a waistcoat to Chapel. May carry a unfurled umbrella or cane and whistle the School song in public.
VI 1 (Oxbridge entrants, Praepostors): As Upper VI, but may carry a furled umbrella.

EXAMINATIONS

External examinations are available on request, and on payment of the appropriate fee. Now that Swinesend has a co-educational Sixth Form, its position in the league tables is steadily improving. This year we hope that our policy of recruiting only the cleverest girls will allow us to join the ranks of the top 250 independent schools in the country.

SPORT

Athletic endeavour is central to the School's life and our goal is to make a man of even the most unpromising and weedy specimen. Four compulsory games sessions are held each week and, although rugby, Swinesend football ('Hackers'), hockey and cricket are compulsory for the first two years, boys are then able to select from a wider range of activities. Swinesend is deeply proud that its darts and snooker teams are the reigning public schools champions.

MUSIC

We have a rich and varied musical life at Swinesend. All boys are asked to learn an instrument (for tuition costs and instrument hire see under 'Fees') and membership of at least one of the School's bands or of the orchestra is encouraged. The bands range from the Swinesend Symphony Pops, chamber ensembles and the Combined Cadet Force Marching Band (described by judges in one recent competition as 'a musical form of shock and awe') to more informal groups, which include 'Wonder Brass' (the Sixth Form Girls' Big Band), a flourishing Folk Club and the High Hats, a barber's shop group formed by School Praepostors.

HEALTH

The health record of the School is remarkable and, despite a brief chlamydia outbreak when the Sixth Form became co-educational, pupils now each spend on average fewer than twenty-eight days per annum in quarantine. The Old Sanatorium now has one fully operational bed and a state-of-the-art management suite.

As inspectors noted in 2005: 'The Swinesend sanatorium defies medical science. We believe some of the cases found there to be unique among schools this side of the Equator.'

DISCIPLINE AND BULLYING

At Swinesend we foster a non-blame culture. There is no need for boys to hide their mistakes. We correct them and we all try to learn from them. We are committed to working with parents to provide solutions for inappropriate behaviour (should it occur). Provided that fees are paid promptly, you will find that Swinesend will provide an ongoing and nurturing learning environment.

There is no bullying at Swinesend. Should incidents of harassment occur on grounds of race, gender, sexual orientation, lack of personal hygiene, political belief or other status, the matter will be referred to the Rev. Winstanley, the School's Diversity Awareness Officer, who will hold an inquiry and seek to address any issues in a non-judgemental manner.

TRADITION

Swinesend is renowned for its picturesque traditions, which have been constantly reinvented over the years. If you decide to send your son to Swinesend, he can expect to take part in age-old ceremonies and customs like Toasting the Simpletons, Dissing the Cold Man and Steg Burning. As a parent, you too will be invited to take part in Founder's Day, on which we celebrate our founder, Sir Walter Ufford, and give you the opportunity to network with other parents.

Of course, all great schools owe their traditions to a long and distinguished history, and Swinesend is no exception. And as no Swinesend prospectus since 1976 has been printed without a summary of the School's history, we once again reproduce it for the benefit of our prospective parents and pupils.

Swinesend: a History of the School

by Mr Charles Edgeson MA (Oxon.) (OS)

In 1540 Henry VIII granted the recently dissolved Abbey of Swinesend to Sir Walter Ufford in recognition of his assistance to the Privy Purse (a down payment of £600 in cash). Finding the dilapidated abbey with its adjoining plague pit to be uninhabitable, Sir Walter endowed the site as a school for the 'education of six sympletones of the town and manore of Swinesende', appointing his indigent cousin – the fanatical Protestant Otway Grundwicke – as Master. Today the School still reserves Foundation Scholarships for six local boys whose intellectual shortcomings are mitigated only by their parents' wealth.

With the accession to the throne of Mary, Sir Walter adapted the School to the fashions of the times and burnt the Six Simpletons at the stake for Protestantism and 'Unnatural Acts'. He then replaced his cousin Otway as Master with the fanatical Roman Catholic Guy Sturge, who was noted for the ingenuity of his pedagogic methods (relics of his apparatus still hang in the Big School).

Sturge's tenure was short-lived. In 1558, to mark the change in educational direction prescribed by Elizabeth I, Sir Walter had him burnt at the stake for 'base Popish Practises'. Otway, who lit the pyre, was reinstated as Master and erected a memorial on the site of the Simpletons' martyrdom. These events are still commemorated each Michaelmas by the tradition of 'Toasting the Simpletons', during which scalding wax is dripped onto the genitals of new boys.

After Sir Walter's death in 1599, Swinesend settled down to nearly 200 years of obscurity, during which the political and intellectual upheavals of the seventeenth and eighteenth centuries left the town and its school wholly untouched. But this was not to last and, in 1790, this tranquillity was shattered by the Great Swinesend Riot. Influenced by the Revolution in France, the misguided Headmaster and laudanum addict the Rev. Benjamin Grundwick preached that a future of intellectual improvement, equality and liberty was near at hand. This obvious nonsense proved too much. Following a particularly provocative sermon in which Grundwick advocated that education should be free for all, the townspeople and pupils rioted, setting upon the misguided schoolmaster and upon each other. In the tumult Grundwick received a blow to the spleen from which he never recovered.

With the School now in ruins and with no pupils to be taught (but with its endowment to be spent) the headmastership of Swinesend became one of the most sought-after in the county. This continued until 1850, when Charles Kingsley led a campaign against the decaying state of the

Relics of Sturge's educational apparatus still hang in the School

buildings, the overgrown grounds and the bawdy house that had opened in the decrepit Chapel. With characteristic foresight, Sir Tobias Ufford, Bt, MP, laid before Parliament 'a Bill for the re-foundation of a School at Swinesend for the education of the sons of Gentlefolk and the suppression of their unnatural urges'.

The new Board of Governors appointed the Rev. Dr Alfred Mudge as Headmaster. Mudge was much influenced by the pre-eminent educationalist Malcolm Arnold, and on taking up the headmastership in 1864 he vigorously applied Arnold's philosophy. Boys were encouraged to suppress their unnatural urges by a rigorous regime of classical music and energetic violin playing. The Head also instituted the forward-thinking system of pastoral care whereby older boys were encouraged to guide younger boys by thrashing them at every possible opportunity when they were not listening to music or fiddling.

Thus equipped for life, Old Swines went out and made their mark upon the Empire. Pre-eminent amongst these was the Hon. Formby Ufford (younger son of the 1st Viscount Swinesend, formerly Sir Tobias Ufford, Bt). Not content with his lot as a remittance man in the Congo Free State, he used his father's money to amass vast wealth by acquiring a 500,000-acre rubber plantation and the State monopoly in hippopotamus-hide whips. Returning to England, he established the Ufford Philanthropical Institute for Fallen Women in Bethnal Green, where, for over a century, Swinesend boys have spent part of each vacation in London's East End enjoying vigorous and beneficial exercise as they receive the gratitude of those less fortunate than themselves. On his death Formby Ufford again remembered the School, bequeathing to it his collection of rubber goods. The Ufford Collection is now on display in the Strongfellow Room.

Mudge retired in 1897. The appointment of his successor, Dr Meredith Bankwell, heralded another new direction for the School. One night in 1908, after dinner at the Athenaeum, Bankwell was told by the Bishop of Gibraltar-in-Europe about the revolutionary *Casa di Bambini* established in Rome the previous year. Much impressed by its precepts, Bankwell asked the name of its founder. Owing to deafness, a surfeit of port and notoriously poor handwriting, Bankwell noted down the name of the founder as Moses Montefiore. Bankwell immediately entered into correspondence with Montefiore (who had been dead for more than twenty years) and soon established Swinesend as England's first Montefiore School — all boys converting to Judaism. By this fortuitous innovation the boys all experienced at first hand one of the character-building activities of early twentieth-century public school education: anti-semitism.

Unfortunately this innovation was shortlived: the whole school was killed on 1 July 1916 after the Officer Training Corps (following the handwritten instructions of Bankwell) embarked on a troop train bound for the Somme instead of its annual camp in Somerset.

The end of the Great War saw a return to more traditional methods at Swinesend. The new Headmaster, F. M. Corncrake MA (Oxon.), began the rapid expansion of the School and opened its doors to a generation of bright young men. One such was the novelist and poet C. P. Branston, who immortalized the School in his affectionate, autobiographical novel *Five Years in Gomorrah*, which was privately published shortly before his departure for the Spanish Civil War. In Spain Branston, remembered by Martha Gellhorn as 'that odious English faggot', joined the Falange Española. Cirrhosis of the liver finally killed him at the Pamplona Bull Run in 1938. The Branston Cup for Poetry is awarded each year in his honour.

With the outbreak of the Second World War, Swinesians were soon to be found in every theatre and the School itself was requisitioned as the Headquarters of the ENSA code-breaking unit. Swinesend, now under the leadership of the new Head, C. X. Tench MA (Cantab.), rose to the occasion; lessons took place in tents on the Fourth XV pitch, the Sixth XI square was ploughed up for a hemp field and the boys took advantage of the men from ENSA billeted in their dorms – learning from them the rudiments of light entertainment.

The post-war world saw the introduction of the Direct Grant, allowing numerous boys from the town's council estates to attend as day boys. While lowering the tone with their poor table manners and rough heterosexuality, their presence led to a period of considerable 'achievement' (with Swinesend winning the Public Schools Snooker Championship no fewer than seventeen times between 1958 and 1976 and numerous Varsity scholarships). But with these unfortunate social changes came upheaval. In 1968 the Sixth Form refused to thrash junior boys; in 1970 the Lower IV would not take part in 'Toasting the Simpletons'; and the following year, the Headmaster, C. L. Stains MA (Oxon.), expelled the entire school when, under the influence of LSD, he became convinced the boys were maggots.

Fortunately, stability has returned since the Government withdrew the Direct Grant, ensuring that the benefits of a Swinesend education are reserved once again solely for the sons of Old Swines and of wealthy businessmen. The School can look forward to another 436 years of proving that, though pedagogical fads come and go, it imprints its own unchanging character on the minds and bodies it nurtures. While there may be other establishments which think themselves smarter or more illustrious, to generations of Old Swines it has been the *alma mater* that has passed on her now unfashionable virtues of decency, moral fibre and 'bottom'.

Floreat Swinesendia

The prospectus drops to the floor as you realize you can read no further. You stare at your bedroom ceiling wondering how your parents could be so heartless as to send you to such a place. The prospectus paints Swinesend life in a rosy light. But is it all true? What is Steg Burning? Is the accommodation really so luxurious? Do the boys in Cockchafer's actually have to have an interest in Scouting? How can you find out?

Ten minutes later you've logged on to the Internet in an attempt to find out what life is really like at Swinesend. Nor are you disappointed. Almost immediately you stumble on a website set up by scurrilous Swinesend boys, where you use your father's credit card to order a very interesting booklet indeed. Three days later you get up early to intercept the postman, who conspiratorially hands you a packet, wrapped in plain brown paper and stamped with the legend: 'Warning: Educational Materials Enclosed'. You rip it open and, inside, you find…

WARNING
EDUCATIONAL MATERIALS ENCLOSED

How to survive Swinesend

An insiders' guide

TREMBLING WITH ANTICIPATION

BURNING TO GET THERE

If you whiled away your time at prep school by perfecting conjuring tricks, learning how to use the flick-knife you bought on the year-group trip to Tirana and looking up rude words in the French dictionary, you might be worried that you won't be able to get into a school of Swinesend's repute.

Fear not: the School values strength of character and potential above all else; and if your father can potentially stump up a bit extra for the Development Fund or School Wine Cellar, then your place on the School Roll is assured.

Before you arrive, be sure to read this booklet to find out what is really in store for you over the next five years, and learn how best to blot out the pain. But when you finally leave your prep school, make sure you do something that will impress your friends who are leaving for rival schools like Winchester, Eton or Ellesmere College, and give them something unforgettable to remember you by. We recommend you show them a magic trick, like this one:

MAGIC FOR BOYS by Jasper Deviant MIMC

An amazing disappearance

Effect   You make your preparatory school disappear in front of the eyes of the astonished spectators.

Secret   You will need the following equipment:

Can of petrol   **Lighter**   **Stooge**

Pour the can of petrol over the more flammable parts of the School. At a prearranged signal, the stooge sets fire to the School while you make your favourite magical gesture. Your friends will be amazed at the effect and you will leave as a hero.

BY THE SEAT OF YOUR PANTS

Every boy is a hero in the eyes of his mother, no matter how ill-deserved the accolade may be. But when you catch her reading the bundle of documents that have been sent to her by the School, do not be misled: she is not shedding tears because you are about to leave home for the rough world of Manhood. No: she has just read the Uniform List and the thought of sewing 1,532 Cash's name-tapes on to assorted items of clothing has left her on the verge of clinical depression.

While your mother is in this state, it is vital that you handle her carefully. Uniform is to a new boy as plumage is to a turkey: it will determine your place in Swinesend's pecking order. Get it right and there will be one less reason for other boys to molest you. Allow your mother to get it wrong and you will be debagged, drubbed and viciously derided.

For this reason, you must resist her impulse to whisk you to the dank, basement rooms of Turncoat & Crapper, the School's London outfitters. She will try to convince you that certain items on the list can only be procured from this emporium: ignore her. What she has in mind – the plastic sports bag adorned with the School's crest, the baggy regulation swimming trunks and the garter flashes supplied in your House colours – will earn you a ferocious kicking if they are seen within five miles of Swinesend.

Remember also that the Uniform List was compiled in 1942. You will not need any boxing kit: the last boxing match was fought at Swinesend in 1971 when R. G. Spokes knocked out and killed T. S. Byles in the seventeenth round. Do, however, insist that your mother buy a gas mask: this is an essential piece of kit after lights out in the Junior Dorms.

Finally, bear in mind that crisp, expensive linen on a new boy is usually viewed as an invitation to pour ink on him. The best way to avoid this is to acquire secondhand clothes. You can do this at the School's Secondhand Shop but, frankly, it's rather a waste of time: when you've reached the end of your first term, all your kit will have been stolen or destroyed, only to be replaced with substitutes found in Lost Property or tucked behind the boiler in the Old Gym. And, happily for your mother, not one of these items will have a name-tape on it to show that it is not yours.

SWINESEND SCHOOL
UNIFORM LIST

1x Winter Blazer (GREY)

1x Sunday Blazer (GREY)

1x Summer Blazer (GREY)

1x Pair Winter Trousers (GREY)

1x Pair Sunday Trousers (GREY)

1x Pair Summer Trousers (LIGHT GREY)

1x Gas mask

1x Ration book & clothing coupons (TO BE LEFT WITH HOUSEMASTER'S WIFE)

2x Shirt Collar (STIFF)

1x Set of Shirt Collar Studs (BONE OR BRASS WITH SCHOOL CREST)

1x Pair Sock Suspenders

1x Pair Gloves (GREY)

1x Pair Spatterdashes

1x Cane (FLEXIBLE, BETWEEN TWO AND THREE FEET IN LENGTH. Praepostors ONLY)

1x Swimming Trunks and Ice Pick

2x Boxing Gloves

1x Cap (Fourth Form Only)

1x Boater (Fifth Form and above)

1x Top Hat (Praepostors only)

1x Tuckbox

1x House Tie (HOUSE COLOURS)

1x Chapel Tie (BLACK, IN MEMORIAM HRH THE DUKE OF CUMBERLAND, worn on Sundays ONLY)

1x School Tie (Worn on Speech and Founder's Day and when outside School grounds ONLY)

2x Chapel Laces (Praepostors ONLY)

1x each of Shirt, Pair Socks, Underpants (GREY)

1x each of Shirt, Pair Socks, Underpants (WHITE, FOR SUNDAY USE)

1x Nightshirt (WITH BROAD ARROW PATTERN)

1x Scarf (Lower School: GREY; Second XV Colours: GREY WITH ⅛" BLACK STRIPE; First XV Colours: GREY WITH ¹⁄₁₆" BLACK AND ¹⁄₂₄" WHITE STRIPE; Praepostors: MAY WEAR PLAIN BLACK, BLUE OR BROWN SCARVES)

8x Football Shorts

8x Football Shirts (HOUSE COLOURS)

8x Football Shirts (SCHOOL COLOURS)

2x Gym Shorts (GREY)

1x Cricket Whites (PALE GREY)

1x Pair Rugby Boots (METAL STUDS COMPULSORY)

1x Pair Cricket Boots

OTC Uniform will be issued by the RSM at the start of the Michaelmas term and is returnable at the end of the school year

EARLY DAYS

ARRIVAL

Dressed in a uniform three sizes too large, you will spend your first
moments at Swinesend standing in the shadow of the School's Gothic
Chapel and watching your father drive your mother over the horizon
at high speed. The memory of his final handshake will be fading; so
too will the scent of your mother's perfume and the echo of what might
have been a sob. You will be surrounded by trunks filled with
ridiculous clothes and a tuckbox brimming with food that you are too
nervous to even think of eating. You will be gripped by a single,
overwhelming desire: to escape.

You will immediately think of forming an Escape Committee with the
other New Boys and of making preparations to dig a tunnel.

After starting a tunnel from underneath the wooden horse in the Old
Gymnasium or from a trap door cunningly hidden under your dorm's
stove, it will only take you a couple of nights' digging to discover that

a layer of impenetrable limestone lies beneath Swinesend's muddy top soil. (Your efforts, however, will not be entirely wasted: your abandoned tunnel can later be put to good use as a handy cache for a couple of packets of Marlboro Golds.)

You may next think of constructing a glider in the attic of your House and flying to freedom. This plan will be swiftly abandoned when you find out that the Corps' RAF section has been trying without success to launch its own glider every Friday afternoon for the last forty years. The strong north-easterly wind which prevails at Swinesend, coupled with the complete absence of any warm thermal current, makes glider-flight impossible.

Finally, you will settle upon the bold plan of acquiring a railway timetable, dressing up as a master and walking straight through the main gate. Put such thoughts from your head: should you succeed in getting beyond the perimeter, you will be swiftly recaptured and returned to the Jug.

The truth is simple: if you are bent on escape, the only way to do it is with the connivance of the Headmaster. You must prove to him that your presence at the School is entirely dispensable. Be prepared to spend time establishing this: only a very rare sort of boy will manage it overnight.

One tried and tested way is to urinate in the Headmaster's food. This was pioneered by Iron Maiden front man Bruce Dickinson when at Oundle, but the enthusiasm with which this method was taken up at Swinesend has made the kitchen staff wary: it will take you some considerable time to gain their trust. Luckily, you will have readier access to illegal drugs; and being found in possession of these is akin to being handed a passport by the Headmaster.

An easier method is to wait a couple of years or so, establish that your presence at the School will cost it more in damaged reputation than it earns from your fees – and then run away. You will find that the School will almost certainly not want you back.

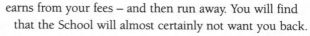

Even so, a boy's parents will sometimes try to prevent a successful escape. Recently the Headmaster sanctioned the escape of Jack 'The Cooler King' Hilts after the boy had clocked up an impressive two hundred and forty-eight misdemeanours over three years, including dosing his housemates with Viagra-laced chocolate, harpooning the Headmaster's dog, attempting to make crystal meth in his study and being caught before 6 p.m. with his middle blazer button undone. The boy's father, however, was not impressed by the assistance which the Head gave his son and commenced legal proceedings, alleging that the escape was motivated by the School's desire to keep its league table position. The court dismissed the allegation when it learned what Swinesend's position actually was and immediately upheld the Headmaster's decision.

SETTLING IN

After ruling out escape and dragging your trunk half a mile from the Chapel car park to your Boarding House and into the dorm you are shown by Matron, you will find lots of bigger and older boys who are willing to show you the ropes. They will do this by prising open your trunk, laughing at the kit your parents have bought (and that no true Swinesian would be seen dead with) and destroying anything useful to hammer home the gravity of your solecism.

When they have finished eating the contents of your tuckbox, your new friends will devote themselves to your welfare and help you settle promptly into Swinesend life. For example, if you make the dreadful mistake of sitting next to the House Captain at tea or, still worse, attempt to speak to him, this helpful fellow is sure to drop by after lights-out and point out exactly where you went wrong.

Even if the House Captain doesn't arrive in your dorm, some of the other boys are sure to introduce themselves and initiate you into communal life. How they do this varies from House to House but in most cases involves a blindfold, handcuffs, whipped cream and a blunt instrument. If you're lucky enough to belong to Cockchafer's, you'll simply have to crawl across a boiling radiator while the House Captain eggs you on with a length of rubber hosepipe. But whichever House you belong to, there is a much more substantial hurdle that you must overcome before you can become a fully fledged Swinesian. This is…

INITIATION

THE NEW SCUM TEST

When Michaelmas comes, older boys will set you an examination to make sure that you have settled in properly and learned all you need to know about the School. This is the dreaded New Scum Test.

In the weeks before you take the test, a boy in the year above will coach you in the right answers. He will have been told that, if you fail, he will have ice cubes poured into his underpants by the Head Boy so he will take a lively interest in your progress: every time you get an answer wrong he will hit you over the head with a Latin dictionary or a cricket bat. There is also an additional incentive for you to learn your lessons: if you get three answers wrong, you will be put in a laundry basket, kicked down the Chapel Steps and forced to take the test again.

There are three things you must learn to pass the New Scum Test:

1. Swinese
When you arrive at Swinesend, you will have difficulty understanding what older boys are saying to you. This is because they make liberal use of the School's own slang, an ancient language that evolved as a substitute for humour. So, in order to help you integrate into the Swinesend community, the first part of your New Scum Test will be an examination in basic Swinese. To help you pass first time, we have compiled this list of basic vocabulary.

Vocabulary needed for lesson 1

Term	Meaning
Bounder's Day	*A date on which OS's who were expelled return to the School. One of the more colourful of their number addresses a select gathering of boys with tips on how best to succeed with the ladies.*
Brandish	*To dangle a junior boy out of an upstairs window by **one** ankle.*
Crem (The)	*The School Kitchens (deriv: crematorium).*
Circle smirk	*An especially gratifying form of shared joke that annoys the master or prefect who happens to be supervising you at prep.*
Cockfondler	*The Praepostor with responsibility for looking after the Headmaster's chickens. As a badge of office, he is allowed to insert a hen's wing into the silk band of his boater hat.*
Dissing the Cold Man	*Originally known as 'Kissing the Cold Man', new boys were expected to kiss the stone head above the entrance to the School Hall. This was supposed to bring them luck. These days the tradition has evolved and boys who fail examinations exorcise their bad luck by hopping on one leg and shouting disrespectful abuse at the figure.*
Dog	*Name for the groundsman's cat.*
Exhibitioner	*One prone to showing off in the showers.*
Fag hag	*An older girl who takes pity on a junior boy who is being given a hard time by his elders and adopts him as something of a pet.*
Fagnostic	*An older boy who does not believe in fagging.*

Term	Meaning
Fivers	*(1) Swinesend Fives. (2) The single-handed game preferred by the Self-Abuse Club.*
George Bush	*A bush on the path leading to the Chapel, normally used to push boys in.*
Gaza Strip	*The long jump sandpit (used by the DOG as a lavatory). Named in honour of Old Swinesian J. C. Gascoyne-Phipps, who captained the Corinthian Casuals in the FA Cup final of 1885 and was disqualified in the long jump final at the first modern Olympics in 1900.*
Glove that dare not speak its name	*An illicit and forbidden boxing match.*
Nanking	*A block of single-study bedrooms, adjacent to the main buildings of St Leger's House. Residents are known as Nankers.*
New San	*The Old Sanatorium.*
Old San	*The New Sanatorium (built on the site of the original sanatorium which was closed after the New San was built).*
Parse bandit	*One who avails himself of your Latin prep without permission.*
School Bill	*(1) The pelican featured in the Founder's coat of arms and featured prominently in the stonework above the main entrance to the Great Hall. (2) Mr William Spragg, an elderly gentleman who loiters around the School gates impersonating a school crossing patrolman.*
Steg Burning	*Each September, on the first day of term, Upper IV boys burn the stuffed effigy of a stegosaurus. Nobody knows why or how this tradition began.*
Skivvy	*(1) A dinner lady. (2) A townsperson (the distinction between the two has become blurred over the years. In practice they are interchangeable).*
Wield	*To dangle a junior boy out of an upstairs window by **two** ankles.*

2. The School Song

It's quite possible that you will learn rudimentary Swinese in a matter of days, but don't slack off the moment you have done so. Many boys leave Swinesend after learning little else except a range of dextrous tricks with a Zippo lighter, a near-perfect imitation of the Headmaster's stutter and the words to the School Song. This last is always the hardest won, but because it's a requirement of the New Scum Test, it's the only one that will make you shed a sentimental tear in later life. Especially if you failed.

The first time you will be expected to sing all six verses of the School Song is at the 'Toasting the Simpletons' ceremony, when you will stand on the old flogging block in the New San while hot wax is poured on to your nether regions. Every time you make a mistake older boys will pelt you with stale biscuits, hymn-books and running spikes before demanding that you start again. After this you will sing it on high days, at sports matches, in Chapel, after Sunday lunch, and (if you are still in the non-swimmers' class after your first year) underwater, so you might as well learn the words now:

The Swinesend School Song

to the tune of 'De Brevitate Vitae'

by C. V. P. Pratt, MC (OS)*

In dark days, England, Swinesend doth
Offer up its precious youth.
In noble deeds and feats of valour,
None can match the Swinesend scholar.

Swinesend, Swinesend, hallowed school,
Childhood home of those who rule.
[Repeat]

The playing fields gave us our strength,
To lead and go that extra length
In punishing the heathen ranks,
On foot, on horseback and in tanks.

Swinesend, Swinesend, &c

No fairer blood was ever shed
Than that the dear old school hath bred;
To dauntless face the cannon ball
And die a credit to us all.

Swinesend, Swinesend, &c

When danger's past, in days serene,
Our noble lads both bright and keen
Tend the fields and lease the land,
To profit from the common band.

Swinesend, Swinesend, &c

In commerce, chambers or the Church,
The lessons taught us with the birch
Make us want to swap our suits
For rubber, fishnets and rare fruits.

Swinesend, Swinesend, &c

And when the final trumpet sounds,
The annual twenty thousand pounds
Secures for every Old Swinesian
A posting to St Michael's legion.

Swinesend, Swinesend, &c

*Pratt was a young master at the School who wrote this song in 1917 in honour of
the members of the Swinesend OTC who perished in the trenches the previous year.
The manuscript was found in his pocket after he collapsed and died on the floor of
a Rouen casino, shortly before the Battle of Arras.

3. The Rules

As well as Swinese and the School Song, you will be expected to know the School Rules. There are many of these but there is only one that can never be broken: only the Head Boy may grow a beard. This is because the sort of boy who would want to grow a beard will never be made a House Praepostor, never mind Head Boy.

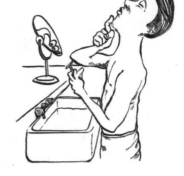

You will also learn quickly that all the other rules that you have diligently learnt are subject to a further unwritten rule: Do what thou wilt shall be the whole of the law (so long as thou doth not get caught).

Once you have passed the New Scum Test, you will be a fully paid-up member of the School community. This means that, next year, you can inflict on younger and smaller boys the same Swinesend welcome.

SWINESEND SCHOOL RULES

RESPECT FOR TRADITION

i.   Boys must not impersonate the School Founder.
ii. Singing in bed is strictly prohibited.
iii. Boys must not pass notes whilst riding bicycles.
iv. Archery is forbidden in the Lower School Yard.

DRESS AND DEPORTMENT

v.   Snowshoes must not be worn in Chapel.
vi.   It is forbidden to wear jeans except in the dark.
vii. Boys must not cut out or otherwise remove the pockets in their trousers.
viii. Only School Praepostors and the School Nurse have the right to place their hands inside other boys' trousers to ensure the above rule is being observed.
ix.   Only the Head Boy may wear a beard. Fringes must be allowed to grow no longer than 1 ⁵⁄₁₆" and partings on the right-hand side of the head are strictly prohibited. Any boy wishing to grow sideburns that extend past the middle of his earlobe must inform his Head of House.
x.   Pupils may not have more than thirteen items of clothing laundered each week, except for members of a sporting first team, who are entitled to a clean pair of socks on the second Thursday after a match.

PRECEDENCE

xi.   The following areas are out of bounds to all boys except for Praepostors: the Upper Boundary, the Inner Circle and the town centre.
xii. Boys may only enter Ring's Piece between the hours of 8 a.m. and 4 p.m., except for Sundays, when it is in bounds between dawn and dusk.
xiii. Boys must not walk on the lawn in front of the Founder's Statue, except for members of the Lower VI, who may use the outer fringes. The centre is reserved for the Upper VI.
xiv. The right to sit on the Lower Wall is a matter of strict seniority restricted to the School Librarian and members of the First XV.
xv.   Boys may only throw Latin dictionaries at masters when the master is not wearing a gown in the classroom.
xvi. Any boy who can recite these statutes in Latin shall be excused punishment for the following offences: smoking, lateness, overfamiliarity with the college servants, beastliness with a boy fewer than three years his junior, and wearing a blue or green overcoat before he has won that privilege.

ROUTINE TORTURE

THE SWINESEND YEAR

Every term, you will be issued with a 'Purple Book'. This publication
contains a timetable you can fill in, a list of all the governors and
teaching staff, the names of every boy in the School (arranged by form)
and, towards the rear, the School Calendar. When you first examine
the latter, you may find yourself wondering about some of the events
that are dotted amongst the termly sporting fixtures and club meetings.
You now know about the initiation ceremonies, but Swinesians
celebrate on many other occasions, sometimes to commemorate some
aspect of the School's history, but usually because boys have been
forced to do so since about 1584.

Carol Service
You may come to the end of your first term at the School worrying that
you still feel lost and alone, wondering if you will ever manage to fit
into School life in the way other boys do so effortlessly. If so, fear ye
not, for Christmas brings tidings of great joy and hope. All you have to
do is join in the chorus of derision aimed at the boy who has been
chosen to sing the treble solo of 'Adeste Fidelis'. In no time at all, you'll
be joining in with your new chums when they brandish this
unfortunate individual by his left ankle and dangle him off the
School bridge.

Shrove Tuesday
The traditional pancake-tossing ceremony was abandoned in the 1970s
after a particularly unpleasant boy, coincidentally named Pancake, took

the title of the ceremony too seriously and left a sour taste in the mouth of many participants: he overenthusiastically wore his fingers to the bone whilst preparing the batter. The day, however, is still noted in the School Calendar, and is marked by an unofficial midnight flour-and-egg fight in which you get the opportunity to batter the boys from a rival House.

The House song contest
The House Shout is a competition with two cups awarded. The first for musicality is always awarded to a girls' Sixth Form House, simply because they have a smaller range of voices to accommodate and thus find it far easier to stay in tune. The second, the far more prestigious Ufford Prize, is judged solely by decibels. Last year's winners, Cockchafer's, gave an especially rousing performance, removing some slates from the roof of the Memorial Hall and even waking Mr Saxby, who has slept through every concert since 1973.

The Maundy Thursday football match
The ancient game on which Swinesend Football is based has been played at the School at least since the 1580s. In those times the game often lasted several days, but it is now played between the hours of

noon and sunset or until one team scores. The whole School is divided into two teams (the Big Chaps and the Little Chaps), both of which are picked by the Head Boy. The Big Chaps score by running the ball into the School Ditch. No one remembers how the Little Chaps score since they have not done so since 1737. A fatal injury happens, on average, every thirty-four years. The fact that it is now forty-three years since the last death ensures that the Maundy Thursday match is keenly attended.

Long Sundays

You will note that one Saturday in every term is marked as a 'Long Sunday'. This is, in fact, a short Saturday and you can go after morning school to stay with your parents or, if they have forgotten to collect you, hang around the School playing Fives by yourself.

Parents' Evening

Some misguided boys might think this is an ideal opportunity to catch up with their parents. It isn't: it's a cruel ordeal for your father. If he is an Old Swinesian, the realization that the same people who taught him are now teaching you (probably using exactly the same lesson plan and books) is liable to lower his spirits considerably. If he is not an OS, and has therefore picked the School in order to give him a veneer of social acceptability, the mere sight of the people employed to teach you might lead him to come away with the impression that he has been wasting his money.

St Dominic's Day

Although you'll be used to attending Chapel every day and twice on Sundays (except during Lent, when the Chaplain is required to enter a clinic), you will notice that the Rev. Winstanley does not enjoy delivering sermons.* However, on St Dominic's Day, the date of the School's foundation, something a bit more substantial is called for.

---

*A typical sermon might run: 'I noticed yesterday that I had a hole in the sole of my shoe. You know, the love of God is a lot like that, except it fills the hole in the soul.'

He will, therefore, choose to warn you against the Sin of Onan by listing all the possible ways in which this transgression can be committed. Many younger boys find this the most instructive day in the entire year. The service concludes with the School's prayer:

Lord, we thankst Thou for our parents' wealth,
Help us strive to grow in strength and health,
Keep us safe from all temptations,
Vulgarity and base inclinations.
Raise us above the common herd
That Swinesend may bear witness to Thy Word.

WATCH YOUR BACK

BEDDING IN

If you hope to survive long enough to experience these highlights of the Swinesend year, you must first learn how to get through a typical School day unscathed. It's a hard-won skill, but the trick – as always – is to offload the pain on to someone else.

All you have to do is make sure you spot the boy most likely to be bullied. This is rarely difficult: he will usually have a ridiculous name such as Simpkins, a faintly northern accent, a father who works in marketing and an unnaturally tidy bed.

A good way of making Simpkins an object of derision is to ask him to help you perform a magic trick in front of all the other new boys.

MAGIC FOR BOYS by Jasper Deviant MIMC

An amazing appearance

Effect   You make a magical gesture and Simpkins appears out of thin air.

Secret   1. Stand with the spectators under an upper storey window. Be careful that you and the spectators are standing on each side and not directly under the window.

2. You have previously arranged for Simpkins to stand discreetly behind the window.

3. Make a magical gesture then divert the spectators' gaze using your favourite method of misdirection (e.g. point at the First XI square and shout, 'Well played!').

4. While the spectators' attention is diverted, a chum (known to professional magicians as a 'stooge') pushes Simpkins out of the window.

Be careful, though. If you make a mess of this, the other new scum will mercilessly taunt you, forcing you to become friends with Simpkins for the rest of your school career. If this happens, he will continually drag you to meetings of the Wargaming Club, vainly hoping that by building up your metal warriors' magical powers you will both feel a little bit better.

PRAEPOSTOROUS CONCEITS

Even if your victimization of Simpkins wins you many friends, don't make the mistake of thinking you are untouchable: you'll soon learn that nothing at Swinesend is more calculated to strike terror into your heart than the sight of School Praepostors pinning up the list of boys they have singled out for punishment. The worst part is the fact that, if you appear on this list, they will glue a copy to the back of your blazer with wallpaper paste.

But who exactly are these individuals who strut through your life with their flapping blue gowns; who, now they are no longer supposed to hit you with blunt instruments or give you 'tin gloves' by running a blistering-hot poker over the backs of your hands, can still put you in Praes' Detention, make you pick up litter or, worst of all, insist you read them a bedtime story?

The Praes are the Headmaster's loyal infiltrators and his hired muscle. Their job is to keep order and, if they catch you committing the slightest infraction of the School Rules, they will subject you to random acts of discipline. So, unless you want to spend a significant part of your School career being forced to eat cold teabags, you need to find out who they are and do everything in your power to avoid them.

The Head Boy

The Head Boy is usually awarded the job because he Sets the Right Example or, in rare cases, is the Headmaster's son. For the first time in the School's history, this year's incumbent happens to be both. Not only does Jack 'Yellowbelly' Taylor display the correct style and impartiality (by, for example, selecting a different member of the Lower IV to polish his shoes each morning), he also displays wisdom.

While the Headmaster, fearful that his son won't get into Cambridge, spends hours completing reams of A-Level coursework on his son's behalf, Taylor is to be found in the Praes' Common Room (otherwise known as the Pigsty) re-cataloguing for the benefit of his successors its extensive collection of photographs of the girls' swimming team.

The Head Girl

When Swinesend's Sixth Form became co-educational, it seemed almost inevitable that a more subtle, gentler touch would soon be brought to bear on the hallowed Pigsty. Accordingly a number of girls were raised to the rank of Praepostoress, given jurisdiction over the other female pupils and asked to go away and set up their own Common Room.

What the Praes didn't bank on was the young ladies' determination to advance their careers. This year, Head Girl Julia Harlech broke several school records by ensuring that the average new girl developed at least two eating disorders, sending more than forty of them to Coventry before Christmas and getting the Sanatorium's stomach pump called into action at least once a week. Her influence has grown so great that when Frognall (Upper IV C) made a mildly ambiguous remark about her legs, he was later found covered in blue paint and strapped to the Founder's Statue wearing only his CCF boots and a sarong.

The Deputy Head Boy and Deputy Head Girl

Following last year's unsuccessful experiment with Lesley Major, the two offices will be separated again.

Captain of Games

Captains of Games, including this year's incumbent, Spelthorne, are chosen by the simple criteria of being the largest, strongest and least intelligent member of their year. But on assuming office they become plagued by the idea that members of the Lower IV, experiencing only two full afternoons of games per week, plus two double periods of PE and athletics training, don't get enough exercise.

Consequently they will devote their every waking hour to looking for boys who have their hands in their pockets, are eating in the street or are wearing turn-ups wider than 1½" at the bottom of their trouser legs. If they catch you committing these offences they will invariably sentence you to Drill, which involves them watching you run round the School fields until either they get bored or you are hospitalized with exhaustion (whichever comes first).

The House Captains

The other School Praes comprise the Captains of each House. They treat their Houses as their personal fiefdoms and you as their personal property. This means you can expect to attend to your House Captain's every whim.

Should his friends in other Houses find you less repulsive than most boys in your year, he will also be liable to send you on early-morning errands to attend to their waking needs as well.

Keep a particular watch out if your House Captain becomes smitten with Jocasta Wadebridge, Siren of the Sixth, or he will send you round to her study every morning with a bunch of roses (for which you will have to pay), and he will invariably order you to lie down in a puddle when she wants to walk across the Quad in the rain.

House Praepostors

Don't be fooled by the House Praepostors. They might be older than you, but they are also irritating and often spend their waking hours dreaming of the day they will be promoted to School Praepostor and acquire a reputation for justice, honour and fairness.

What these boys will not tell you is that every boy in his final year at Swinesend is made a House 'Polly'. Since there is no dignity in the rank, you may safely ignore it, unless its holder happens to favour forbidden and traditional methods to exert his power.

The Cockfondler

The boy who holds this historic post (see Swinese) has just a few ceremonial responsibilities – such as polishing the length of rubber piping with which Praes maintained discipline until the fall-out from the notorious 1971 'Omérta' court case (which saw R. G. Spokes, Captain of St Leger's, sentenced to seven years for manslaughter after beating a boy to death). Unfortunately this leaves this year's incumbent, Walkinson, with plenty of time on his hands, which he mostly spends inventing new traditions.

If Walkinson suddenly decides that members of the Upper IV have no right to blow their noses in front of the Founder's Statue, you may be certain that he has also devised cruel and unusual punishments for boys who are caught flouting this rule – such as locking ten of them overnight in one of the three grace-and-favour study bedrooms that are a perk of his office.

Fagging

When you come to Swinesend, you may worry that you will be asked to fag for a Praepostor. Don't: those days are long past. A Polly today will simply rely on any passing junior to give him a hand. Just keep your ears open when you're wandering near the Sixth Form Common Room.

Fag! Fag! Faaaaaaaaaaaag!!

Yes, Fulthorpe?
Don't speak to me until I say so, you little scrot. Now get on with these questions. I need to untie Wilson in a couple of minutes.

Sorry Fulthorpe. What is a fag?
You are, Epwood.

Why am I a fag, Fulthorpe?
Because I am in the Sixth Form and you are in The Shell.

What does a fag do?
What I tell him to do.

Why must I do what you tell me to, Fulthorpe?
Because that is the way it has always been done at Swinesend. When you are in the Sixth Form you will understand these things. Is there anything else?

Yes, Fulthorpe. Sorry, Fulthorpe. What is your bidding?
Wake me up! Fetch me some ink and paper! Get me some buttered ale and custard tarts! Warm my lavatory seat! Take this

message to Springling! Cook my sausages! Make my tea! Fill my
bath! Stoke my fire! Polish my candlesticks! Tidy my room! Save
me from drowning!

Save you from drowning, Fulthorpe?
Yes. In the 1870s, when a senior boy fell into the River Swine, no one
came to his aid when he shouted 'Help!' so he tried 'Fag!' instead.
Immediately one dived in and rescued him. You get the idea.

Thank you, Fulthorpe. Which shall I do first?
None. There's something else I want you to do, Dolly.

Sorry, Fulthorpe. Yes, Fulthorpe. Why did you call me 'Dolly',
Fulthorpe?
Because you are so good-looking. In this school you get a girl's
name as well as having to perform all these little services. You will
receive your reward next time you bring me my morning coffee in
the shower. Now, come here: there's something I want to show
you.

Hang on a second, Byles told me that fagging had been abolished at
Swinesend. Has it, Fulthorpe?
Well, technically, the little creep is quite right. Officially, you have
to do the communal chores like lunchtime litter duty, cleaning the
lavatories in the House changing rooms, and polishing the Bursar's
Lexus. But, worse luck, I still have to supervise you doing all that,
so I might as well ask you to carry out a few personal favours.
Ex officio, you understand. Now, pop off to the corner shop and
buy me twenty Bensons.

I'm sorry, Fulthorpe. If fagging has been abolished, I don't think...
Ouch! Why did you just hit me, Fulthorpe?
Because I can.

STICKY SITUATIONS: HOW TO AVOID CLOSE FRIENDSHIPS

If you find yourself suffering at the behest of your elders, it's not uncommon to yearn for a special chum who will offer you a helping hand in times of trouble. Unfortunately, the boys who are the most likely to do this are also much older than you, leading to a few awkward moments when their demands of friendship become just a little too insistent.

The warning signs that an older boy is trying to form a close friendship with you are not always easy to spot. If you play for the Colts Second XV and he's always on the sidelines chanting your name, how do you know he's not just an avid supporter of House sports? If he's a Praepostor who is always making you spend time on your knees or bent over his desk, he may just like an extra clean study.

It's best to be on your guard, though. To avoid suffering from regular and potentially embarrassing nuisances, you should refuse any invitation from an older boy to do the following:

- Join him for a cigarette behind the Fives court after dark.
- Accompany him on a yachting expedition to Norway.
- Head off into the woods with him to search for badgers.
- Practise your Fives technique.
- Join him and a group of chums for a board game in his study.
- Meet up with some friendly locals in Corby's municipal lavatories.

Be warned: these precautions are not always enough to prevent you forming a close friendship. But it will help you enormously if you know whether you're the sort of boy who is vulnerable to an older boy's approaches: if you are, you can try to steer clear. The table overleaf will soon tell you what sort of boy you are.

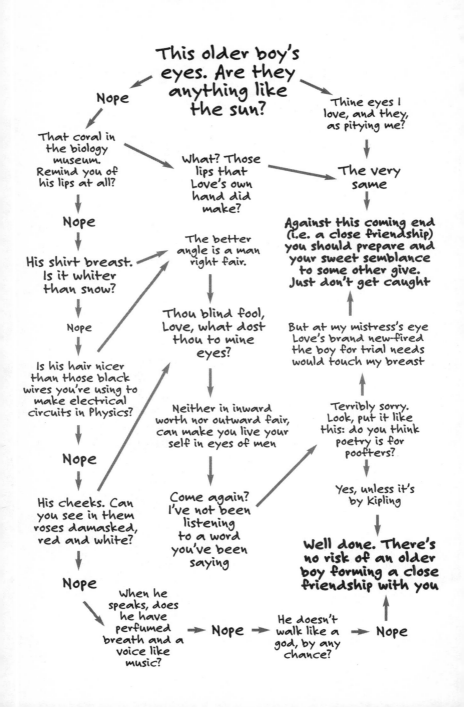

THY ROD
AND THY STAFF

IN LOCO PARENTIS

If you think older boys excel at making you feel uncomfortable, then you'll soon discover any adult employed by the School is in an altogether higher league.

Take for example the School Nurse. A gnarled Scotswoman in her early sixties who is nicknamed 'Auld Beaky', this woman is famously uninterested in whether you have a mild sniffle or a full-blown case of scarlet fever. What interests her is Hygiene and, when she's not patrolling in the Sanatorium, you will often spot her hanging around the Lower IV urinals as you go about your business, putting you off your stride by making prurient insinuations about the smell.

You'd be much better off turning to your House Matron, who will clean your clothes, dispense sympathy and be like a second mother to you, but with the added advantage of not complaining about your manners or telling embarrassing stories about your childhood. Just don't push her too far, though: the recent scandal involving Cockchafer's matron, the Captain of Games and the backscratcher demonstrated that decades of pent-up maternal yearning can express itself in dangerous, unpredictable forms.

Then there's the School Marshal, R. G. Spokes. An Old Boy of the School, who in his day was House Captain of St Leger's, Spokes was given a job by the School authorities on his release from prison in 1978 and is now Swinesend's most feared employee. Spokes's primary job is to summon boys to the Headmaster's study or to the Praes' Common Room when required.

But he has other duties: he collects the attendance registers each morning, fences goods through the School's Secondhand Shop, and visits the town's public houses, turf accountants and massage parlours each afternoon in the company of the School Praepostors to check that Swinesend boys are not playing truant.

But the most distressing staff member of all is your Housemaster. You might have thought that this man, who is paid to look after you, would make some effort to put you at ease or to take an interest in what you do. Not so: you must remember that he is also your surrogate father and, as such, will seek to avoid any awkward or emotional moments. He will do this by ignoring you as much as he possibly can. (The only exception to this is Dr Udall, Housemaster of St Leger's, who is more than likely to invite you to join him in a one-on-one session on his couch on which he will pat your knees, shake you by the shoulder and ask you if are having any problems with girls.)

If your Housemaster does force himself to speak to you, it will be a sign that he has just learnt that your work is not up to scratch, that Simpkins has told him how you sneaked into his study to decant the contents of his drinks cabinet into a hip flask, or that he has just crept up on you in the dorm at the very moment you were doing a hilarious imitation of his wig falling off.

More rarely, you will be ushered into his presence because you have done exceptionally well. Then, just like your real father, he will be all too happy to bask in the reflected glory. Just don't fall into the temptation of telling him that you only took the last three wickets in that all-important House match because you had smeared Deep Heat inside an opposing batsman's box, or that you only noticed the old lady's house was on fire because you were busy luring her terrier into the trap you had constructed in the garden. If you do this, he will haunt you for the rest of your time at School, popping up whenever you least want him to be there. What's worse, he's likely to encourage his colleagues to join in the fun.

THE MASTER RACE

Permitted to hire whom it likes, and teach what it likes, Swinesend School attracts men of brilliance who, whether they specialize in History, Divinity, Chemistry or Greek, spend their days trying to comply with the founding statute that decrees masters should not be 'drunkards, whoremongers or lewd in living'. Some manage it, others don't, but attaining two out of the three is generally deemed to be satisfactory, if not admirable.

In the Swinesend staffroom the cult of the amateur prevails, and any master found to hold professional qualifications is dismissed with a haughty sneer. In a stroke of luck for you, almost every teacher is also likely to share your contempt for external examinations and league tables, preferring to play to his strengths before a captive audience of boys.

So, next time you are sitting in an English lesson and your schoolmaster discards *King Lear* and instead tells you the best way to fight off a Zulu war band armed only with a string of sausages and an assegai, remember that he is trying to bestow on you that elusive hallmark you will not receive elsewhere: the character of a true Swinesian.

Wisdom
Of all the qualities that a good schoolmaster seeks to impart, one of the most important is wisdom. And the highest form of it comes from some of the dictates of Swinesend's most venerable teachers.

Generations of Swineseians will remember the kindly advice offered by Careers Master Dr J. Tyler, who is even now fond of telling his favoured pupils (with a leer), 'What you need is a big black woman' or advising Sixth Form girls 'not to bother with a career. All you really want to do is get married and have babies.'

Of course, it is the Headmaster who is the wisest of them all. When you finally leave the School, he is sure to give you the following sound advice: 'Always remember that you are a Swinesend man and behave accordingly. If, for instance, you are invited to someone's house for the weekend, you must always clean the bath.'

Single-minded endeavour

Swinesians are renowned for their refusal to be swayed by popular opinion, as you will learn from the Physics Master, Dr Creech, who never lets changing circumstances sway him from his original purpose. When you and your classmates arrive late at the labs after your morning swimming class, you are sure to find Creech in full flight, busily instructing an empty room.

Knowing one's duty

The Latin Master, W. H. Harrison, will take pains to impress this quality on you. On those not infrequent occasions when he spies a bird landing on the window ledge of his classroom, he always waits patiently for it to fly away before remarking, quite rightly, 'I am not paid to teach pigeons.'

Self-reliance

As a new boy at Swinesend, you will quickly learn that, sometimes, you will need to do things for yourself. Mr Fell, the Head of English, is a keen advocate of this approach and will often barricade himself in the Olde Cripple Inn, a disreputable public house in the nearby village of Ufford, for a week at a time, leaving you in your classroom to get on with it.

Standing up for yourself

The greatest honour any boy can achieve is to be challenged by his teacher. Some, such as M. Clarenceux of the French department, will simply invite you to race him round the Quad, threatening you with detention if you fail to win.

But Mr Polk, the Head of History, prefers a more complex approach. If you question him over some of the trifling errors of fact he sometimes makes (such as confusing the Italians with the Arabs), or impugn the honour of Baroness Thatcher, Polk is apt to pull down one of the sabres which decorate his classroom and challenge you to a fencing match.

If this happens to you, do not worry: he will always provide a bowl of clean water to wash away any blood that might be shed in the course of the contest.

Behaving like a Christian

If nothing else, the School Chaplain, the Rev. Winstanley, is a convinced post-modernist who not only seeks to understand other world religions, but strives to make sure that Divinity lessons are 'relevant' to young Swinesians. For instance, he may ask a boy in his class to crawl across the floor with a spoonful of water clamped in his mouth and instruct the others to kick him if any water is spilt – a most lively way of showing how Jews have been persecuted over the ages.

Younger boys will be given a relatively gentle introduction to the horrors of Sin with stories about the awful doings he claims to have witnessed in Berlin's nightclubs. Older boys are told the story of his ordeal at the hands of the Mau Mau in Kenya and his most famous lesson, given to members of the Lower VI, and involving a gnu, a bacon slicer and a half-ton of iron filings, is never forgotten by anyone who has heard it. This is not to say that he does not take his spiritual duties with the utmost seriousness. For instance, if he believes a girl is wearing a skirt that is too short, he will make it his duty to measure the length of the offending garment daily, if needs be, until he is satisfied.

Stiff upper lip

No one likes a boy who blubbers, and few like him less than Mr Buchanan, the Games Master. Most boys can cope with running around in the mud, tossing a rugby ball to each other as he yells, 'Treat it like a hot potato!' But if you're the sort of boy who drops balls, Buchanan will throw one into your face as hard as he can. And if you so much as whimper he'll take you inside and make you jump over a six-foot vaulting horse until you either stop crying or land on your kneecaps.

Lofty ideals

These don't come loftier than the ones held by D. T. S. Wilson, who, at the age of sixty-three, is the youngest member of the Geography department. You may be mostly interested in where he buys those string vests that you can see through his polyester shirt, but he will not regard such enquiries as important. For him it is far more essential that you learn how to convey ideas of the greatest importance, such as the outrage he feels at colonial bishops being denied representation in the House of Lords. Boys who point out that such clergymen are now in short supply are likely to be rewarded for their tedious dedication to facts by the sight of Wilson brandishing a stuffed crocodile called Tamburlaine.

Endurance

One of the most effective weapons the masters possess is their ability to paralyse you in a state of extreme boredom. It may be that, after you have spent hours staring at a complex equation you cannot understand, or have been forced to transcribe Vergil's *Eclogues* over the course of an afternoon, you will feel more than equal to coping with whatever tedium life throws at you.

But you will be wrong. It is only when you have sat through double English under C. J. 'Steggy' Kenman, completing a mindless comprehension exercise about the Chiltern railway line for the second time in as many years, that you will become perfectly equipped to endure any intellectual privation.

Is *your* teacher a dope fiend?

🌿 Is he socially isolated and withdrawn?

🌿 Does he guard his privacy intensely?

🌿 Is he sometimes violent and threatening, either physically or verbally?

🌿 Is his behaviour unpredictable?

🌿 Is he plagued by constant money problems?

🌿 Is he forever reaching for the perfume, cologne, deodorant or mouthwash?

🌿 Does he leave the classroom frequently or lurk in the staff room or other out-of-the-way locations during break time?

🌿 Is he incoherent?

🌿 Does he display symptoms of depression, feelings of hopelessness and/or helplessness?

🌿 Is he sloppy or unkempt in his personal appearance?

These are all signs of *substance dependency*. If your teacher displays any or all of these symptoms, he may well be a *substance abuser*. Substance abuse is an *addiction* and a *treatable disorder*. Through treatment that is tailored to individual needs, your teachers can learn to control their condition and live normal, productive lives. But they will need help. They will require counselling, psychotherapy, support groups or family therapy. They will need medications to suppress the symptoms of withdrawal and drug-craving and in blocking the effects of drugs.

NB: These signs are also the symptoms of being a teacher in a minor public school. This condition must not be confused with that of being a schoolmaster in a major public school, the symptoms of which are delusions, hallucinations and unrealistic expectations of life, and for which there is no known cure. The only treatment which provides some remission for the sufferer from the minor public school malady is the regular ingestion of large quantities of alcohol.

LITTLE LEARNING

THE BORES OF PERCEPTION

After a couple of weeks at Swinesend, you will soon discover that one lesson is very much like another.

You sit at your desk, the door opens, you stand up: a strange man enters the room, gown flapping, and muttering something that could be 'Sit down', 'Sedete', 'Asseyez', 'Sitzen' or simply 'Grrnk'. You then spend the next forty-five minutes watching this man talk, as your mind ponders Life's Big Questions: what cup-size is Matron's brassiere? Why isn't my tool as big as Simpkins's? If I were invisible, which girls' Boarding House would I visit first?

But what if your teacher asks you a question? You will need to find out quickly what lesson you are in. It can prove a painful experience to answer a question from your History Master with a description of the life-cycle of a tadpole. But it's no use looking to Simpkins at the neighbouring desk for help: even if he knows what lesson you are in, the chances are he'll think it funny to let you flounder.

To help you avoid such awkward situations, we have created a Ready Reckoner. Paste it into the front of your Rough Book and, if you are suddenly hauled back to reality by an insistent schoolmaster, you will know at a glance what lesson you are in – and the worst he can accuse you of being is stupid.

SUBJECTS OF INDIFFERENCE

Once you have established where you are, a further danger awaits: the
timetable. According to this document, you are allowed five minutes to
move from one lesson to another, which is little help when Maths
finishes and you have to sprint for ten minutes to reach the languages
block. Nor does it help you when you race out of French and are
forbidden from hailing a taxi to take you to the new Sports Hall a mile
away on the other side of town.

This can cause great inconvenience and a typical day will expose you
to a series of irate masters who insist on keeping you behind to make
up the time you lost by arriving late for their period. By evening, you
are liable to miss supper altogether while Dr Creech insists you
undertake an hour-long experiment which, properly speaking, you
have only fifteen minutes to complete.

The smart boy will, therefore, not allow himself to be controlled by his
timetable: instead he will take control of it. Once you realize that every
year the same masters are given the same classes at the same time, all
you have to do is select lessons that will allow you to saunter from
classroom to classroom at your own pace. You can do this by doing
badly in class and dropping down to a subject stream that is
timetabled at a more convenient time and place.

For example, on Wednesdays, something like this should suit you
very well:

8.50 a.m.: English (C stream)
The older members of the English department, most of whom
experimented with hallucinogenic drugs in the late 1960s, will
encourage you to start the day by getting in touch with your inner self
and exploring your awakening sexuality by close textual analysis of the
works of R. D. Laing and the *Bulldog Drummond* series. The younger
masters, however, prefer traditional methods of teaching and will make

you memorize Browning's *Pied Piper of Hamelin*. If you enter their classes forewarned with the knowledge that Hamelin Town is in Brunswick and that the river Weser (deep and wide) washes its walls on the southern side, you will enjoy a period of peace.

9.25 a.m.: History (A stream)

These days, no schoolmaster knows anything about the past, unless it's something that happened during the Tudor era or the Second World War. After three years of study you will be tempted to draw glib parallels between your time at Swinesend and (1) the Nazis and their love of order, discipline, violence, cult of athleticism and fetish for uniforms and/or (2) Elizabethan England's love of torture, close male friendships and tobacco. Fight this temptation: it will have occurred to every other member of your class except Simpkins. If you really want to learn something useful from history, dip into the press archives to find out the name of every master who was asked to leave another school and demand a king's ransom for your continued presence in the top class.

10.00 a.m.: German (D stream)

At Swinesend you can study either French or German for at least three years and leave school not knowing how to order a meal in a restaurant. You will, however, learn to ask directions to almost any town hall on the continent and know all the swear words in those languages. More advanced students will also learn that foreigners prefer to swear in English because it is a far better vehicle for obscenity. A far more obscene sight, though, is the spectacle of Herr Teufels, the German Master, leading a lesson on *Musikkultur* and trying to get his lips round the words 'Vaughan Williams'.

The best thing about studying languages is the foreign exchange programme, during which you get to stay two weeks with a boy from another country. You will also be able to meet girls throughout this period and try out your language skills on them. Unfortunately, unless they are particularly lewd or have a deep fascination with town halls, you are likely to risk a slapped face. But don't worry – the family you stay with will have been carefully chosen because of their ability to speak perfect English, so you shouldn't get into too much trouble.

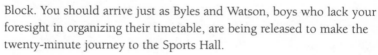

10.30 a.m. – 11.00 a.m.: Morning break

A chance to saunter over to the Science Block. You should arrive just as Byles and Watson, boys who lack your foresight in organizing their timetable, are being released to make the twenty-minute journey to the Sports Hall.

11.00 a.m.: Double Science (B stream)

When your science teacher tells you it's possible to make LSD from hydrochloric acid and nutmeg, this is just a joke designed to prove the supremacy of Darwinian principles. Any boy who is sufficiently interested and enterprising enough to act on the advice will naturally be selected for expulsion.

12.10 p.m.: Maths (E stream)

Do not expect to learn anything useful here. If you require mental stimulation, calculate the probability of the School's best mathematician committing suicide or being jailed for drug dealing while at university.

1.00 p.m. – 5.00 p.m.: Lunch followed by Games

5.00 p.m. – 6.00 p.m.: Double Geography (F stream)

All you have to do is draw round stencils of Great Britain and, for some reason, South America, colouring in levels of rainfall, principal exports, or regional variations of unemployment as desired. Remember that the man who teaches you this subject will care deeply about one thing: whether or not you write in pencil or draw in ink. But don't worry: although he knows it's important, he can't actually remember whether it's pencil you should draw in, or ink. That said, he's still convinced that British Guiana remains part of the Empire.

OR: Double Classics (A stream)

Studying Classics gives you both clarity of thought and the opportunity to look up rude words in TWO new languages. By the time you enter the Classical sixth, you will be able to command a large vocabulary, which can be used to refer to unspeakable acts without shocking either the Chaplain, your parents, or even yourself.

Without wishing to spoil your fun, here is just a handful of words that you can find in Liddell & Scott's *Greek Lexicon* and Lewis & Short's *Latin Dictionary*, both of which are in the School Library.

ῥαφανιδωσις	thrust a radish up the fundament
bumammus, -a, -um (*adj*) [*deriv* bu-mamma, having large breasts]	of the vine, with large clusters
πορνοβοσκεω	waste one's substance on harlots
cinaedus, -i *m*	He who practises unnatural lust, a sodomite, catamite
cunnus, -i *m*	the female pudenda

inguen, -inis *n*	a swelling in the groin
irrumo, -avi, -atum	to give suck, to treat in a foul and shameful manner
pudendus, -a, -um (adj)	of which one ought to be ashamed
τριβας – αδος – ἡ	a woman who practises unnatural vice with herself or with other women
mufrius, -ii, *m*	a term of abuse
πηριν – ινος, ἡ	scrotum
masturbator, -is *m*	one who defiles himself

Now that your appetite has been whetted, use the dictionaries to find as many rude words as possible and jot them and their meanings down in the spaces below. It's fun, isn't it?

....
....
....
....
....
....

A SUPER IDEA
Why don't you and a chum have a competition to see who can find the rudest word in five minutes?

Form order

If you fear that you are doing too badly, or even too well, to stay in the desired stream for a certain subject, fear not. You will be alerted to the danger by a slip of paper which your form master will hand you each fortnight. It will look something like this.

SWINESEND SCHOOL
FORM ORDER

Name **Lampson, Oliver**

Form **LIV**

Subject	%	Position in Form	Effort (++/+/S/-/--)
English	23	25	- -
Mathematics	2	24=	- -
Latin	14	22	-
Divinity	99	25	- -
French	0	25	- -
German	43.4	19=	S
Physics & Chemistry	9	23=	-
Biology	6	3=	+
Art	16	21	S

Average %: 24   Overall position in form: 24=

This is a Form Order; and what's more, it's a bad one. With results like this you might attract attention. To stay in the correct stream and to avoid the wrath of your schoolmasters, the jeers of your swottier classmates and the disappointment of your parents, you should aim for largely average results. The mark you are awarded for effort is a matter of personal taste and, if you are in the A stream for a particular subject, you might even indulge yourself by aspiring to come top of the form whilst retaining a double minus for effort.

But how are you to achieve this seemingly impossible task? Luckily, there is one way to improve your grades sufficiently. By cheating.

What is cheating?

After your master hands out the Latin vocab test and settles down to some scholarly research with the *Racing Post*, you might see Byles Minor pull out a small piece of paper with a lot of little scribbles on it. The furtive chap hides the note in his fist, but soon takes it out again. Peeping back and forth between the dozing master, the test and his crumpled crib sheet, there's no mistaking it – Byles is *cheating*.

Cheating in a game is *foul play*. For instance, if you hide the ball under your jersey in a game of Swinesend Football and pretend that you haven't, this is cheating. Pretending something is yours when it isn't is called *theft* (unless you are a master in which case it is called 'confiscation'). Copying someone else's work and saying its yours is a special type of cheating called *plagiarizing* (say: play-jeh-rize-ing).*

Why cheat?
The answer is simple. The cheat can fool around instead of studying for that Latin test and still get good marks.

Is cheating wrong?
Silly people often frown upon cheating. They believe that a boy who cheats needs to talk with his schoolmaster and his parents so they can find some 'solutions' together and that 'talking about these problems and working them out will feel better than cheating'.

---

* This sentence and much of this article has been plagiarized (play-jeh-rized) from the thoroughly worthy site http://kidshealth.org/kid/feeling/school/cheating.html. Only the meaning has been changed.

It is not surprising that such muddled thinking has caught on when you are examined on 'coursework' and have easy access to the 'Internet'. Cheating is now *too easy*: for as little as £50 you can purchase an essay written by *a teacher* and, with a little adaptation, pass it off as your own. Worse still, the advent of the photocopying machine has resulted in whole examination papers being reproduced and offered for sale in advance of the examination for as little as £400.

Proper cheating, however, fosters both self-reliance and ingenuity (as well as boosting a school's performance in the dreaded league tables). But cheating is not only a means to these ends. Like all crafts, when performed well, it is a joy in itself.

What are the best ways to cheat?
Those which remain undetected.

MASTER BAITING

Unfortunately, if a schoolmaster suspects you of cheating, he might start developing an unnatural interest in you. He may even make a habit of summoning you to the staff room at morning break or inviting you to spend time with him when school is over.

If this begins to happen, it's possible that the master is nurturing a vendetta against you. From the first suspicions of cheating, he will move on to thinking that it's his duty to victimize you because you never do your prep, never get your hair cut and are always the boy who organizes the underarm farting competitions in his lessons. You, of course, will be adamant that he hates you for being cleverer, funnier and crueller than him. That's why you'll get him back by...

Treating him like a hero

Nothing will make a master back off quicker than finding that a boy idolizes him. Make a poster of him and sport it on your dormitory locker. If he runs the birdwatching society, enrol without delay. If you're really brave, ask him for extra tuition. Your relentless presence will goad the man to near madness, but he won't be able to lay a finger on you. Highly recommended.

Studying extra hard

Not to get good marks, but to bombard your foe with questions about arcane details of his subject. He will not have studied it in depth since university, so opportunities to humiliate him abound.

Ringing him up

Take the master's mind off you by giving him something else to think about. Seek out a local telephone box, ring him up, put a handkerchief over the mouthpiece and inform him that the copy of *Whipping Boys III* or *Young, Dumb and Well Hung* has been sent to the Common Room as ordered. Or why not pretend to be from another school that wants to offer him a better job and a massive pay rise? With luck, he'll hand in his notice the next morning.

Spreading the word

Try asking the Chaplain (in confidence and on behalf of a friend) what one should do if one were to see the master kissing Simpkins. Soon he'll be on everyone's lips.

Writing his letters

Take charge of the master's correspondence. Write to a range of his favourite charities and offer substantial donations in the name of the School. You will soon find he loses interest in you as he attempts to convince the governors he was the victim of an impostor.

Go out with his daughter

This will madden him beyond all things. Even if you do nothing more than hold hands on the way home, he will imagine that you are doing all sorts of unspeakable things with her. If he attempts to put a stop to this, it will only make the girl keener on you and guarantee a more protracted period of torment for him.

But if all else fails…

Get expelled by someone else

It will deny him victory and, if a colleague whom your schoolmaster hates boots you out instead, you will leave Swinesend triumphant.

QUESTIONS NEW BOYS ASK

Teachers' pets

Whatever you do, never try to curry favour with a schoolmaster. It will have unexpected and undesirable results.

What is a teacher's pet?
An animal or other being for which a schoolmaster harbours an intense affection. Sometimes it will be a dog; now and then it will be a cat; and in rare instances it will be an orange-fronted hanging parrot.

Can I become a teacher's pet?
No.

Should I ever look after my teacher's pet?
Under no circumstances. Take as a cautionary tale the boy in the
Upper IV who agreed to look after the Art Master's pet owl during
an exeat. He took it home, gave it a perch in his own bedroom,
fed it chocolates, read it poetry, introduced it to next door's rabbits
and sang it lullabies at bedtime. The owl died. The master was
inconsolable. The boy was blamed for not feeding it. Only after
much protest and pleading could the grief-stricken teacher accept
that the bird had pined for him and thus died of a broken heart.
Don't let this happen to you!

If I help him get rid of his pet, can I replace it in his affections?
Even if he says he is getting tired of his cat, don't believe him.
Once the local press finds out that you stuck his cat in a sack and
threw it into the House Pond, he will deny all knowledge of your
actions and blame you for all the trouble it has caused him.

Is it wise to give my teacher a pet?
No! And if you really must, don't give it to him in person. Many a
boy has left under a cloud after going on camp and presenting a
sheep to his master by putting it in his tent. At Swinesend, animal
spirits get a boy nowhere.

EXAMINATIONS

If you believe that examinations are an irksome, if necessary, test
of what you learned during a preceding term, you are quite wrong.
They exist simply to provide masters with a rare opportunity to play
together.

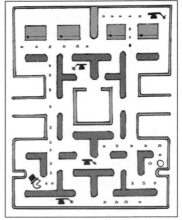

You may also think that you are
forced to sit six feet away from
Simpkins so that you can't copy his
answers. Again, you are wrong:
without wide aisles between your
desks, no schoolmaster would be
able to play *Invigilation Pacman*.

The Swinesend version of the game
is simplicity itself. One master takes
on the role of Pacman. The others are
ghosts. The ghosts must capture
Pacman, and Pacman must move in and out of the aisles between the
desks as he attempts to evade them. It is easy to work out which
masters are ghosts as they invariably attempt to capture Pacman in a
pincer action. Any suspicions will be confirmed when three or more
schoolmasters converge on the same spot and only one of them is not
smiling.

Clever boys will seek to influence the course of the game by asking for
extra paper at strategic points of the action, luring ghosts to a far
corner of the hall. This will gain boys credit with Pacman but may
cause frustrated tutting and the fretful twisting of gowns amongst the
ghosts. That said, it is worth remembering that if you ask Pacman to
escort you to the lavatory, you will win that master an additional life
and the power to destroy any ghosts that cross his path within the next
sixty seconds. And if you do that, he may just overlook the matter next
time you fail to do your prep.

GOD MOVES IN MYSTERIOUS WAYS

CHAPEL

At Swinesend, boys are often told that 'to work is to pray'; so most boys treat the time spent in Chapel at the beginning and end of each day as a welcome respite from both. Fortunately, because the School is staunchly Anglican, little is expected of you in these services except that you mumble a few responses and kneel at the correct moments.

Do these things by all means, but remember also that the House of God is a place of sanctuary in which the masters cannot touch you. This fact alone gives you Heaven-sent opportunities to indulge with impunity in activities like these:

1. Singing
Tedious services and hymns can be enlivened with a good bellow. Extra fun can be had when you change, mispronounce or simply reinterpret the words to various hymns. Classics such as 'Rank By Rank Again We Stand' or 'For We Like Sheep' set the benchmark.

2. Starting a card school
Some boys see all that kneeling and bowing behind the stalls as the ideal opportunity to catch up with their schoolwork unobserved. If you are more ambitious, you might play a game of cards with a chum, agreeing beforehand that the loser will have to do the winner's prep. To help avoid detection, simply murmur 'Amen' whenever you wish to raise the stakes.

3. Torture

If you were unable to finish your prep the previous night because Murray kept sticking his compass in your leg, you will have been praying for a chance to wreak your revenge. Chapel is the answer to your pleas: it gives you the perfect opportunity to elbow Murray in the small of the back, give him a wedgie or superglue his knees to the floor. He won't want to draw attention to himself so, Christ-like, he will suffer in silence.

4. Ogling

The best seats in Chapel are in the gallery and, when one of the girls' houses is seated directly below, they are hotly contested. Get one of these pews and the temptation to stare down is one that few can resist. Be warned, though, that the perfect view offered of Jocasta Wadebrige's cleavage on one occasion last year caused several impetuous juniors to lean too far over the balcony. For the neophyte this is paradise enough. The more experienced boy, however, will realize that there is greater pleasure to be had in watching Jocasta Wadebridge's discomfit after he lets a note flutter down to tell her that her bra strap is visible.

5. Organ grinding

Boys like Simpkins will be rewarded for their hours of twiddling with pipes and stops by being offered the chance to play the School organ during Morning Service. You will be rewarded by the inspiration of placing various balloons on top of the pipes and soap suds inside them. Simpkins simply will not understand why so many boys are sniggering throughout his performance.

6. Tomb sealing

One of the Chaplain's odder customs is to begin his Easter sermon from within a large box, only to emerge at the moment of resurrection. For a truly life-affirming gift, you should take the opportunity to liven it up even more.

Last year a couple of boys from Cockchafer's took the opportunity to staple down the lid. As usual the service began with the Chaplain's voice booming out from the box, 'Jesus dies! He is entombed! On the third day... He rises from the dead!' only to deviate from the script with a *thud*. 'Rises from the dead!' *Thud*. 'Rises!' *Thud*. 'Rises!' before lapsing into a stream of most un-Christian language which only subsided when the Chaplain was overcome with emotion and had to be rescued by the RSM.

7. Converting to Islam

If the service is a particularly boring one, and if all else fails to divert you, stand up in the middle of it and shout out the formula 'Ash-Hadu Allaa Ilaaha Il-lallaah Wa Ash Hadu Anna Muhammadar Rasullulah'. Congratulations, you are now a Muslim. This will cause your chums great merriment and the School authorities will not dare touch you.

FOOD FOR THOUGHT

School food

As the Chaplain will frequently remind you, 'Man shall not live by bread alone, but by every word that proceedeth out of the mouth of God [Matthew IV:4].' However, some new boys worry that even bread will be in short supply, and inedible at that. We hope the following will answer any questions you may have about the quality and frequency of school food.

Will I get fed?
Yes.

Is the food good?
No.

Can I complain to my parents?
Yes, but they will ignore you. They are, after all, paying for you to experience some ancient character-building traditions, and bad food is one of the most jealously guarded.

Boys have been known to parcel up their school meals and send them home for inspection; but in the wake of recent legislation restricting what may be sent by post and the death of several sniffer dogs, this is no longer recommended.

I don't mind rotten food, but I need lots of it. Will I get enough?
School inspectors have cottoned on to the fact that some public schools still teach boys how to fend for themselves by the simple expedient of not giving them enough to eat. Fortunately, the Headmaster's Rottweilers have prevented so much as a single inspector reaching the Swinesend kitchens, so you will probably still have an empty stomach and plenty of scope for food-related fun.

Fun?
Yes, by finding enough to eat without getting caught. You can break out of bounds and head to the local chippie or Chinese takeaway, where you will soon find that forbidden fruit is the sweetest. Even better, ask your parents to send you extra food in boxes labelled 'sports equipment'. With a few tins of *pâté de foie gras*, the odd cake from Fortnum & Mason, or a Cadbury's Creme Egg, you can not only keep body and soul together but bribe the other members of your House to do your prep, beat up your enemies, polish your shoes or, if the bribe is a very substantial one, be your friend.

What happens if I can't afford my own food?
Then you will have to perform various little personal services for the other boys in exchange for the odd sticky finger.

My services are not much in demand by the older boys. What should I do now?
Steal.

SWINESEND DISHES

As new scum, you will be required to dine daily with eight other boys in a 'mess'. One of these is called the Server. His job is to help himself to all the best food. Another one is called the Vice Server. His job is to throw you scraps.

Scraps worth eating are rarely come by. But once in a while the Vice Server will grab a potato wedge or a slice of apple tart and shout: 'Quis?!' Your job is to stay alert for this moment and shout 'Ego!' as quick as you can. If you bark it out quicker than the other boys, you get to eat the titbit. If you don't, you have to eat the same muck as everyone else, namely:

1. Porridge
Affectionately known as 'two lepers sharing a bath', Swinesend porridge has no taste, is impossible to swallow and causes great inconvenience to the laundry skivvies if you pour it down Simpkins's trousers. Luckily for Simpkins the stuff is never hot, or he really would have something to cry about.

2. Sausages
There's no swine like the swine
in a Swinesend sausage,
When a Swinesend sausage
hasn't one per cent swine!

Such is the refrain to the song boys
have sung since the late 1980s, when a
Lower IV pupil sent a school sausage to his scientist
father to analyse, only to learn that the banger contained less than one per cent meat. Neither is there reason to suppose that the little meat in the Swinesend sausage is pork, although the sight of one has been known to make even the most omnivorous boys consider converting to Islam, Judaism or, in extreme cases, vegetarianism.

3. Bread

'Surely there's nothing they can do to the bread?' you ask. You expect it to be dry. You're even prepared for it to be stale. But what takes you aback is the wholly unexpected carapace of grease, pitted with black flecks that look suspiciously as though they started life up the nose of the snuff-addled Woodwork Master. On the plus side, you can have lots of fun feeding this sort of bread to the ducks, which will then sink to the bottom of the pond, never to resurface.

4. Custard

Swinesend custard is served as a sealant for spotted dick, treacle pudding and jam roly poly. Sporting boys turn their bowls upside down at the end of their main course and take bets on how long it will take for their pudding to submit to the laws of gravity, break through the custard and land on the table. The record is held by Mainwaring-Thomas of the Upper IV who, after being made by a witty schoolmaster to hold his bowl upside down during afternoon school, kept his pudding in place for four hours, fifty-three minutes and twenty-two seconds.

5. Cheese

The local Swinesend blue is much praised by connoisseurs. Indeed, many parents make a point of buying a truckle from the local cheesemonger after they've dumped you and your luggage at your Boarding House. Just don't expect to see this delicacy on offer at the School: what you are given is a waterproof, rubbery, glow-in-the-dark horror that is guaranteed to induce in you dreams of Mr Cobley the Maths Master dancing round your bed clad only in a purple cloak and a velveteen jockstrap. Deeply disturbing.

6. Fresh fruit

Now you're just being silly. The only fruit at Swinesend is in tins: and that's kept on the shelves of the masters' nuclear bunker, forty feet under the cricket pavilion.

MENS SANA IN CORPORE SANO

SPORTING ENDEAVOURS

Swinesend food may contribute little to a healthy body, but the School does not neglect its duty to give you plenty of physical exercise. If you are the sort of boy who reads poetry for fun and is capable of abstract thought, the five winters you will spend at Swinesend, knee-deep in mud with the wind whipping round your extremities, are designed to straighten you out. You will be expected to play one or more of the following games every day. But remember, *on no account practise or show too much enthusiasm*. This is almost as unsporting as studying hard or displaying an interest in the Arts.

Hackers or Swinesend football

The School's own game, Hackers, is preferred to soccer. Features such as its seventeen players against twelve, six points for every opponent lamed and a set of rules that vary according to the length of the shadow formed by the junior boy who is acting as the attacking side's goalpost make it a tough but character-forming game.

Rugby football

Rugby is only played in the summer when there is insufficient mud for Swinesend football. Because of this, competition is usually restricted to House matches. Remember that if you spend the entire match charging at the short, fat, slow boy on the wing, or use each ruck to stamp on the short-sighted halfwit who is making up the numbers in the second row, you will avoid having to face the more talented players on the opposing side. This will help cement your role as a valued member of your team.

Cricket

Since this is a team game, do your bit to keep up morale by displaying the right sporting spirit by, for instance, enjoying a cigarette whilst fielding at deep fine leg or studying the racing pages whilst waiting to go in to bat. If you are at the crease, ignore all fast balls as being unworthy of a gentleman's attention. Members of the First XI are expected to provide their own dirt to scuff up the ball.

Cross-country

No Swinesian worth his salt aspires to joining the School cross-country squad: even people who like sport think it is pretty stupid to run long distances through muddy fields on bitingly cold winter days. This is the preserve of lanky, queer-looking fellows who, when not panting their way through the School's woods, spend their leisure hours in the IT suite debating the finer points of Red Hat Linux.

On the other hand, the annual Ufford Run, in which the whole School participates, is one of the highlights of Swinesend's sporting year. It has never been cancelled for inclement weather. Held across ten miles of the surrounding countryside, much of which has been redeveloped into either industrial units or trading parks, many outsiders wonder how anyone ever completes the infamous course. The answer is simple: the local farmers and patrolling security guards object virulently to the presence of any outsiders and, labouring under the illusion that the competitors are 'pikeys' and burglars, threaten to shoot any stragglers.

Hockey

No amount of boasting about being hit in the face by a stick or stopping a ball with the more sensitive parts of your anatomy will convince your fellows that this is not a sport for girls.

Fives

Fives is a sort of squash played without a racquet. Never mind the Eton version which was played between the buttresses of the Chapel wall; forget the cruder Rugby variety; and on no account play the *arriviste* Gresham's game, which is simply the Eton variant with a back wall. Swinesend Fives is the purest sporting contest imaginable as it is now played without a front wall (as it no longer exists: it was knocked down in 1958 when the Old Library was demolished to make way for the town bypass).

Swimming

Swinesend is the only public school to uphold the tradition that swimming is strictly a winter sport. A proposal to heat the Old Pool was resisted by the Swinesend Ice Skating Club, which shares it.

Walking to nowhere in particular

At Swinesend, every boy Must Take Exercise Under Official Supervision. So if you have lost your swimming trunks, had your games kit stolen or broken your arm, you will be ordered to walk around the athletics track all afternoon in order to satisfy the official requirement for supervised exercise. Devotees of this sport can spend years perfecting either a purposeful stride or else a jaunty, hands-in-the-pockets swagger.

Cage fighting

In the past, boys who yearned to strip to the waist, cover one another in oil and exploit each other's vulnerabilities had to meet in strange, hidden places at odd times. Nowadays, thankfully, they can simply use the School's new cage fighting facility. Already, the sport is one of the most popular with boys and the annual Masters v Boys (Under-16) fixture is proving a real hit. Swinesend also hosted the first-ever Girls' Public School Championship in this sport, which broke the record for the highest attendance at a school sports fixture.

Because the cage was built with lottery money, the facility is open to members of the public on occasional evenings during the school holidays. Next term we are looking forward to our first Town v Gown fixture and the First Team has already started training by hanging around Corby's Market Square on Saturday nights.

PLAYING THE GAME

Whatever sporting pastime you find yourself forced to do, you'll soon discover that there's a lot more to Games than trudging around the playing fields on the pretext of keeping fit. Indeed, you will quickly learn that it is not the winning that matters; neither is it simply the taking part. What matters is the impression of effortless superiority you stamp on your opponent.

If you lose, your opponent must be made to feel that you are morally the winner because you displayed such superior sportsmanship. But, should you actually win, your foe must be left in no doubt that his own failure is no success at all.

You should start to make your opponent feel inadequate even before the game has started – indeed, if you are expert, you can do it when arranging a match. Consider, for instance, the manner in which Swinesend avenged its bitterest-ever defeat – all without a single ball being bowled.

The Schools, Swinesend.
February 27, 1866

Dear Sir,
I write to ask if a match between Westminster
and Swinesend can be arranged for this season?
The most convenient date for us would be any day
in the week beginning June 17. We shall be happy
to play on any ground in London which you
may select.

Yours, etc.,

J. Spencer Phillips,
Capt.

Westminster

March 5, 186[6]

Sir,

The Captain of the Westminster Eleven is sorry to
disappoint Swinesend, but Westminster plays no school
except Public Schools, and the general feeling in the Schoo[l]
quite coincides with that of the Committee of the
Public Schools Club, who issue this list of public schools —
Charterhouse, Eton, Harrow, Rugby, Westminster
and Winchester.

Yours truly,
E. Oliver, Capt.

Spencer Phillips, however, put Oliver firmly back in his place the next year by refusing even to repeat the invitation. Since that time Swinesians have quietly refused to represent their country at any sport that has ever included an Old Westminster in the team.

When facing a technically superior team with whom a match has actually been fixed, you need to adopt a slightly different approach.

Swinesend's fencing team did this when Brentwood School arranged a fixture against them. Although the Essex boys bragged of being regularly crowned Public Schools' Fencing Champions, we demonstrated our effortless superiority by the simple expedient of spending an afternoon wandering around Brentford in Middlesex. The message was clear: a Swinesian cannot be expected to know where any town in Essex is, let alone sully his name by competing against boys who are at school there.*

The best way to guarantee success, however, is if you play games that no one else does. We used to play the Tudor game of Real Tennis and, as there are only about forty courts in the world, always boasted a 'world class' team. The game was too easy, however, and Swinesend gave it up in the 1920s, when Canford School was founded, installed its own court and tried to challenge us to a match. Of course, the best way to ensure that no one can beat you at a game is to invent the rules yourself. In doing so, you will follow in the footsteps of…

Revd J. D. Hutchinson:
Accidental inventor of modern football
The School was the first to systematize the rules of football and the Swinesend code (known in the School as 'Hackers') is still played today. The man responsible, J. D. Hutchinson, Housemaster of St Leger's, aimed to divert his boys' unwholesome urges, believing that

*Eton copied exactly the same tactic the following season.

they would never again indulge in impure behaviour when they could instead grapple with each other on a muddy field in winter and stamp on each other's most sensitive organs.

Hutchinson based the new sport on the School's ancient game, which was played each Maundy Thursday. This lasted three or four days (often without a ball) and severe injuries were common even among spectators. The Housemaster brought order by limiting the game to three halves of two hours each and introducing ten rules (based on the Commandments) to regulate the boys' behaviour.

Hutchinson hoped that all schools would, in time, adopt the game and arranged a fixture against Rugby to promote it. Sadly, Hutchinson had neglected to clarify the rules on hacking. After thirty minutes, the Rugby players were bleeding badly and decided to leave the field of play. When their captain – who was one of the few boys still able to walk – picked up the ball, the enraged Swinesend team chased him the length of the pitch and wrestled the ball from his grasp before raking him with their studs.

Within a few years, however, Swinesend's defeated opponents had discovered the fun to be had from inflicting similar carnage on other schools and claimed the game as their own creation.

SWINESEND'S SPORTING HEROES

*Hutchinson was not Swinesend's only sporting pioneer and, as
you graze on cucumber sandwiches in the Pavilion after a school
match or stand in assembly in the Great Hall, your gaze may
wander to the portraits of the School's other athletic heroes.
Not only did they make their mark on Swinesend itself:
they impressed it on the sporting world at large.*

B. J. T. SMITH (1880–1915)
BATTING FOR BRITAIN

The School's famous cricket field, the Upper Waste, was the setting for many of the game's most celebrated feats. The world record for the longest innings with no score (three days, eight hours and fifty-two minutes) was set there by B. J. T. Smith in May 1897 and is unlikely ever to be broken.

One of Smith's team-mates was the celebrated First World War general Sir Anthony Wrykin, who, although he was bottom of the Science stream four years running, liked to say that he had learned all he needed to know about life and war on the Swinesend playing fields. Sadly, his decision to send a slip cordon alongside the German lines at the Second Battle of Ypres proved fatal to Smith, who went over the top armed only with a cricket bat ('ready,' as one survivor noted, 'to knock the Boche for six'). Fittingly, Wrykin's statue now stands in the car park that was built on the Upper Waste in 1995.

FRANK MUNN (1982–)
THREE TIMES WORLD CROSSBOW CHAMPION

World Champion while still at school, Munn first discovered his unique talent when, in Lower IV C, he shot the Senior Groundsman's lurcher. Suspended for a term, he returned to school a crack shot and subject to an ASBO banning him from Northamptonshire's council estates, where he had taken to stalking exotic pets such as snakes, crab-eating monkeys and pit-bull terriers. In later life, he went from strength to strength and, last year, received the ultimate accolade of topping the RSPCA's 'Most Wanted' list for his insistence on using real bulls' eyes whenever he practised.

PERCIVAL LAVENDER
(1902–87)
SPORTING COLOSSUS

The name of Percival Lavender needs no introduction to followers of the fortunes of England's 1930s Rugby Union team. The School Pavilion boasts an unrivalled collection of this 23-stone behemoth's sporting memorabilia, including his trademark squirrel-fur jockstraps, ball-shaped Vaseline jar, sharpened steel studs and the special shirts with stirrups attached to the hem that he used to give to visiting players (all generously left to the School by his close companion of many years, local coiffeur Mr Jason Slingsby). Today's sporting heroes owe him a debt of gratitude following the recent sale of a set of ears, which he bit off after his opponents made fun of his name during the 1919 England Schools trial. The proceeds have allowed the School to invest in world-class facilities such as weight rooms, laboratories and specialist equipment to allow boys to practise stamping and gouging.

COL. RUPERT BARNES (1959–)
THE FILTHY CHUKKA

Barnes, who has represented England at Polo twenty-seven times, is best known for being the first player ever to be sent off at Hurlingham after he trained his horse to perform a sliding tackle and brought down the Prince of Wales's mount during a tournament in 1993. To show there were no hard feelings he later offered to 'take the Prince's wife off his hands'.

Married six times, he has been deported from Argentina four times, horse-whipped on the steps of the Travellers Club twice and appeared in one reality TV show.

A LUST FOR LIFE

In addition to its Fives courts, unheated swimming pool and an armoury filled with rusting sabres, epées and foils, Swinesend has a pack of impeccably bred beagles.

Eton has one. So too have Marlborough, Stowe and Radley. Unlike at some other schools, Swinesians have always ignored the fox and put their hearts into killing hares. It is a happy sport which provides excitement to all participants equally.

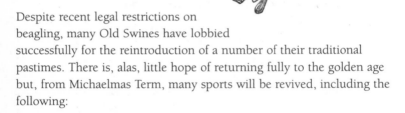

Despite recent legal restrictions on beagling, many Old Swines have lobbied successfully for the reintroduction of a number of their traditional pastimes. There is, alas, little hope of returning fully to the golden age but, from Michaelmas Term, many sports will be revived, including the following:

Throwing at cocks
Shrove Tuesday, as well as being the day on which pancake-tossing took place, was long a fixture in the School's sporting calendar. In former times, as at many public schools, boys would stuff a cock into a pot or tie it to a stake by a short cord. The trick was to kill the bird outright with a skilfully thrown broomstick. Not as easy as it sounds, though; and, as a writer for the *Gentleman's Magazine* noted, it was often dangerous to be near the target.

Duck and owl hunting
Have you ever tried hunting ducks with dogs? Even if you have, it is unlikely you will have ever experienced the extra fun that can be gained by tying an owl to the duck's back. Those who have read

School match accounts of this sport, now stored in the Jowell Learning Centre, will remember that, when the dog gets close, the duck dives, inspiring the owl to claw it. As soon as the petrified bird resurfaces, the half-drowned owl, still clawing and now hooting horribly, sinks its talons into the duck and causes it to dive once more.

Ram hunting

The ram hunt is an old Swinesend tradition that Eton borrowed for its festivities on Election Saturday. In the early days, boys at both schools would hunt a ram to death. This continued until an animal escaped across the Thames and ran into Windsor Market, with a mob of Etonians in hot pursuit. The locals failed to see the funny side of this unfortunate accident so, from about 1740, a compromise was reached: henceforth the ram was instead ham-strung and 'knocked on the head with large, twisted clubs'. This version lingered on at Swinesend until 1964 and many Old Swines have fond memories of it to this day. Indeed, the Old Boys' club hopes to send a team along to Eton when the sport is revived next year.

Boy-roasting

Evelyn Waugh (Lancing), a keen observer of public school life, once remarked that when boys 'were not roasting fags' they 'roasted snared pheasants over open fires'. This was certainly the case at Swinesend and, although Health and Safety legislation nowadays makes pheasant roasting tricky, scorching is coming back into vogue. The poet Southey (Westminster) remembered a boy whose schoolfellows 'used to lay him before the fire till he was scorched, and shut him in a trunk with sawdust till he had nearly expired with suffocation'. No Swinesend boy would ever leave such a job half done.

Torture

As William Makepeace Thackeray (Charterhouse) once put it, 'Torture in a public school is as much licensed as the knout in Russia. It would be ungentlemanlike (in a manner) to resist it.'

The knout, a kind of whip with rawhide thongs and (sometimes) hooks, never really passed into general usage at Swinesend, but in common with 1840s Harrow there is a particularly fun game for boys who don't keep up at football – cutting large thorn sticks out of the local hedges and then using them to flog the miscreants until the blood pours down outside their jerseys. The school is confident that the first group of J. Edgar Hoover Memorial Scholars to arrive from the States will enjoy a revival of this extraordinary tradition.

Jew-baiting

Boys with foreign-sounding names have long provided sport for their fellows at public schools. This pastime was in danger of dying out at Swinesend which, like Clifton College in 2005, has closed its House reserved for Jews. Fortunately the opening of the Swinesend Islamic Centre (established thanks to the generosity of many Old Swines from the Gulf States) should allow this age-old pastime to continue. Pogroms are held on the third Saturday of each month during term-time.

Cripple-taunting

This sport remains popular at many rival schools, including Abingdon, where Radiohead's Thom Yorke generously provided hours of entertainment with his paralysed left eye – his fellows tormented him continually with cries of 'Salamander!' A pastime that is bound to enjoy a vogueish revival here at Swinesend.

Swot-swatting

Some quarry simply needs to be put out of its misery quickly and humanely. Swots like writer and Newdigate prize winner James Hamilton Paterson (King's School, Canterbury) are a case in point: he used to weep in class when asked to read Tennyson's *Morte d'Arthur* aloud. 'Boy,' he later remarked, 'did one get bullied and mocked for weeping at Tennyson.' At Swinesend we throw bricks and the collected letters of Philip Larkin at repulsive little snotfaces like this.

Fag-bashing

This quarry can belong to one of two species (though they are pursued by similar means). The first is in the shape of the younger boy who warms your lavatory seat in the morning and prepares the crumpets for study parties. You may beat this type of fag for slacking, but you must never kill him: it will inconvenience you.

If, on the other hand, the species you are tracking is a 'homosexual', he is fair game. This sort of person will provide you with hours of wholesome sport. If the quarry escapes from the School, however, it is no longer lawful to hunt him.

Swinesend Boys should mark what happened to a few Old Uppinghamians who, in 1994, found that the actor Stephen Fry had turned up for a reunion. They forgot themselves and could not resist the chase, accusing him of being 'anti-monarchist, anti-public school, communist and homosexual'. As a consequence, two were fined for assault and affray, proving once and for all that a lust for life is no childish pursuit, but the work of a lifetime.

First Aid for Boys

At Swinesend, fags who get bashed get little sympathy. Boys and staff alike much prefer to take a typically no-nonsense attitude to illness and injury, rather like Sir Robert Bruce Lockhart, a public school man who lived well into his eighties. 'As a cure for the cold,' he used to say, 'take your toddy to bed, put one bowler hat at the foot, and drink until you see two.'

Although bowler hats, if not strong drink, are in short supply at Swinesend, it is sensible to prepare oneself against injury or an outbreak of illness. The School Nurse can't be everywhere at once so, if a chum in Middle Dorm poisons himself by eating undercooked rat, your fag gets friction burns in the back passage, or someone gets speared by a carelessly thrown javelin, they are much more likely to welcome your intervention if you have a working knowledge of First Aid.

Just be sure to wash your hands after reading this.

Plague

Plague, whether bubonic, pneumonic or septicaemic, is a revolting affliction in a schoolboy. The only positive thing to be said about the ailment is that its sufferers tend to die within five days of contracting even the mildest version of the three. Luckily, a sharp-witted boy may effect a cure before the disease is fully upon him.

Diagnosis

If you spot swollen lymph nodes in the neck, armpits or groin of another boy, then the chances are he has the bubonic version of this grotesque lurgy. When in doubt, grope his liver or spleen and check for enlargement. Pink or red sputum is often a sign of the pneumonic variety. If he has septicaemic plague, then he will almost certainly be beyond hope.

Cure

Tobacco. As ever, Eton followed Swinesend's lead by making smoking compulsory to ward off the plague outbreak in the 1660s. This cure was stringently applied: one Etonian 'was never so much whipped in his life as he was one morning for not smoking'. Swinesend boys, however, have never needed such an incentive and the School has remained plague-free to this day.

Syphilis

Syphilis has been a long-standing problem for curious Swinesians, especially the sort whose first (and probably enduring) love is, in the words of Southey, likely to be 'some street-pacing harlot'. Indeed, the School authorities have always taken an interest in the issue, with the headmasters of Eton, Rugby and Swinesend appearing before the 45th meeting of the Royal Commission on Venereal Diseases as recently as 1914.

Diagnosis

If you spot that a boy has chancres, or skin ulcerations, on his penis or rectum, or that the lymph nodes in his groin are swollen, he may have early symptoms. If in doubt, wait a bit longer (one to six months): if he really does have the disease he will develop a reddish rash on the trunk and extremities, whilst mucous patches may appear on his genitals or in his mouth. If you wait long enough, tumour-like growths, Argyll-Robertson pupils,* spinal deformities, insanity and death will follow.

*This is nothing to do with Mr Argyll-Robertson's form in the Lower IV, but refers to a disease of the eyes.

Cure
Invite the sufferer to join the Sixth Form Arts Society, where his overwrought visions of deliquescence and delirium amid the bohemian society of the East Midlands are certain to be a huge success.

Original Sin

Every Swinesian will be prey to this disease at some time or another and, unless treated promptly, symptoms may linger for upwards of one, two or even three decades. In extreme cases, the sufferer will never be saved from the pernicious effects of the malady.

Diagnosis
The onset of this illness is usually preceded by a fall, although its incubation period varies wildly from individual to individual. The sign to look out for in a boy is, quite simply, wilful and unexplained disobedience. In extreme cases, the sufferer will refuse to carry out the wishes of an older and more vicious boy.

Cure
Caught promptly, Original Sin may be washed away. Hold the sufferer by the ankles, lower his head into a lavatory bowl, and flush until he attains a state of grace. He will struggle at first, but after repeated immersions, his countenance will soon become white as snow.

Love

This is essentially a spiritual malady, but no less hazardous for that. It can turn otherwise healthy young men into trembling milksops. If left unchecked it can undermine morale with disastrous consequences on the games field.

Diagnosis

Who is that figure alone and palely loitering? Can it really be Barnes, once the pride of the Second XV back row? Is he off his food, does he alternate between moments of introspection and attempts to claw the walls of his study? Has he lost all joy in life? Does he even forbear to administer summary punishments to the Lower Dorm? The chances are that he is smitten with love for a girl (or one of the members of the Lower Dorm).

Cure

There is no known cure. In severe cases, transfer to another school is the only option.

THE SANATORIUM

Don't for one minute imagine that a life-threatening disease and a sad demeanour are all that is required to ensure a pleasant day tucked up in the San untroubled by French irregular verbs or the House cross-country competition.

Even if your acting abilities are good enough to trick an inexperienced young master, they will certainly not impress the School Nurse. With her practised eye, she will see through your ruse and within minutes you will be back at your desk or puffing round the School fields in mud-spattered running shorts.

It will take you many years to acquire both the learning and the ingenuity that will earn you more than a couple of days in the Sanatorium. Even after many hours with your Housemaster's medical dictionary you will not approach the greatness of Swinesend's most successful malingerer, Edgar Thripp, who in 1963 not only spent a month in the Sanatorium but had the whole school closed down for six weeks after simulating the symptoms of anthrax.

But do not be disheartened. With practice, you will learn to simulate symptoms that will baffle Nurse long enough for you to miss a couple of hated lessons or a House match. This at-a-glance guide provides you with all you need to set you spluttering on your career as a successful malingerer.

Symptom	The School Nurse's diagnosis	Induce by...	Pros	Cons
High temperature	Influenza	Sucking hard on a mercury thermometer (this will result in a false reading)	Simple to perform	This old ruse is well known to Nurse. If you fail to convince her, she will insert the thermometer elsewhere
Dizziness, headache	Concussion	Asking Byles why he is such a turd	The Nurse will believe you	You will have concussion
Blindness	Beastliness	Reading *Railway Modeller* magazine after Lights Out	Harmless	Nurse will prescribe a cold shower
Shivering, vomiting, convulsions	Malaria	Consuming seven pints of snakebite and black	Inducing the symptoms has pleasurable side-effects	Pricey
A limp	Serious psychiatric disorder	Shooting yourself in the foot with a .303 Lee Enfield rifle	Guaranteed to keep you off Games permanently	You will incur the wrath of the RSM for wasting ammunition

THE CALL OF DUTY

THE CORPS

If your experience at Swinesend so far has left you feeling quite alone and tempted to listen to Marilyn Manson records, then you will tick off the days until you receive your call-up papers for the Combined Cadet Force. From the moment you sign up at the outset of the Upper IV, you will be expected on parade every Friday at 1400 hours sharp, when Regimental Sergeant Major Nails will subject you to a regime of small arms drill and shouting that is designed to mould you and your schoolboy comrades into a crack unit of trained killers.

But even if you're the sort of boy who has moral or aesthetic objections to spending a day each week in military uniform, you'll lose them the moment you consider Swinesend's only alternative to the martial life: Community Service. Opt for this and you will find yourself forced to visit some housebound and semi-senile old fantasist who will not only force you to cut his lawn with a pair of nail scissors while he rebukes you for not joining the Corps, but will also bore you with immensely dreary and wholly fictitious tales of how, if he hadn't sneaked off to see action with a syphilitic French tart in Normandy during 1944, he wouldn't have lived to be the only surviving member of his battalion.

Compared with such horrors, the hardships of CCF life are extremely attractive. But if you want to make sure that you get the most from your time in the Corps, you must plan your career with the utmost precision. To do this, you simply need to make sure you don't forget three things:

1. Avoid RSM Nails

A former regular with the Swineland Fusiliers who retired with the rank of Corporal after twenty-four years' service, Regimental Sergeant Major Hamish Nails is in day-to-day charge of the Corps; in practice this means Nails spends Monday to Thursday selling 'Army Surplus' goods from the storeroom, dropping into the Sanatorium to test the springs of the daybed he has lent the School Nurse, and ticking off boys who return kit which they claim to have outgrown.

But the moment he dons his uniform on a Friday morning, Nails becomes a different man: feared by both boys and masters alike, he rules the parade ground with a rod of iron and strives to make miserable the lives of public school, officer-class types like you. And while he will tell you that his *nom de guerre* was 'Hard Ass Nails', woe betide anyone who refers to him as anything but 'Sir'. If you fail to do so, he will take it as a personal insult on a par with suggesting that he can't hold his drink or reads poetry for fun and he will make it his life's mission to reduce you to a snivelling wreck. On average this takes about twenty-six seconds.

The only boys to whom Nails shows any semblance of warmth are the senior NCOs, with whom he shares whisky in return for the

How to attack a tree

1. *Identify a suitable tree*

2. *Wait under cover until dark*

3. *Attack tree at speed from all angles*

opportunity to regale them with military anecdotes. Whilst this sounds fun, after hearing about the time he garrotted a Malay communist with a bicycle tyre and stories about his sexual escapades in the garrison towns of West Germany, you will long for the obscurity of the ranks where you will face nothing worse than the prospect of spending an afternoon lying face down in a rain-filled ditch and expending an inordinate amount of energy attacking inanimate objects, such as trees.

2. Survive basic training

Basic training introduces you to military life. Failure to pass will result in you being deemed to lack moral fibre and will lead to instant dismissal from the Corps and immediate transfer to Community Service.

The two terms in which you undergo basic training are the most arduous you will ever experience. Every Thursday night you will spend three hours rubbing Kiwi Parade Gloss into the toecaps of your boots, safe in the knowledge that the next afternoon will see them stamped on by a scrofulous Fifth Former who insists that you call you him 'Sar'nt'. This individual will then scream at you and your fellow recruits as you stamp your feet to the left (in threes), then quick march you to a hut in which he will show you how to strip apart a .303 Lee Enfield rifle that last saw service in Waziristan. While this is happening, console yourself with the knowledge that boys who become too enamoured of the military lifestyle will most likely be seeing service in Waziristan in a couple of years or so.

3. Find a cushy billet
Once you have survived basic training, you must take particular care when choosing which arm of the Corps to join. You will be given a choice of the following.

The Infantry
If you think that the martial life of the Infantry is for you, you will realize your mistake when you discover that you are expected to iron three pairs of trousers – lightweights, camouflage and dress – every week. This is because the infantry is the personal fiefdom of the RSM, who never announces what you should be wearing on parade until six minutes beforehand. Get it right and you'll spend the afternoon bayoneting straw effigies of Nails's rival bed mechanic and competitor

Method of tying feet.

for the School Nurse's affections, Chief Petty Officer Bathurst. Get it wrong and it's the Number 1 Field Punishment for you.

The Royal Engineers
Under the command of Science Master Major C.P.E. Binns-Wolff, most of your time will be spent rallying the forces of engineering against what he believes to be the forces of Socialism and Anarchism, and what you know are really boys from the neighbouring town. You will

do this by digging defensive trenches and sharpening spikes to stick at the bottom of them. Unfortunately, thanks to the Headmaster's realization that the only boys stupid enough to impale themselves also happen to be his pupils, you will also spend every Friday evening removing the stakes you so painstakingly laid only hours before.

The RAF

The glamour of flight is much overrated and you will spend most of Friday afternoon in a classroom discussing aerodynamics before failing to launch the School's antiquated glider with a large rubber band. On the rare occasions you take to the skies on a trip to a local aerodrome, it will be in a creaking 1930s biplane piloted by a terminal alcoholic with more in the way of moustache than brain cells. He will delight in putting the plane into a

'Cocaine,' he said tersely.

death spin above the School cricket grounds and will only pull out of it when he can read the scoreboard.

The Royal Navy

The putative pleasures of dressing up as a jolly Jack Tar and hanging around naval dockyards in tight clothes are more than outweighed by the tedium of knot practice and memorizing the whole of the *Naval Ratings Handbook* (1951 Edition). Not that you will ever see a dockyard: as a member of one of the public schools furthest from the sea, the only water you will spot will be in the local gravel pit where you will learn to sail your Topper.

Intelligence

This unit is run by Colonel Rodderick, RA,* the officer commanding the Corps and the School's Assistant Art Master. Most Friday afternoons start off with an attempt to map the topography of the School but this is soon abandoned in favour of producing rather fetching watercolours of Corby's historic, winding streets. Membership of this unit is only by the personal invitation of the Colonel.

The Rifle Team

If you can get into the Corps Rifle Team, little will be required of you other than that you lie on your belly and point your weapon in the right direction.

The Royal Marines

Boys who are especially keen on bloodshed and suffering can volunteer to endure several days' worth while they attempt to pass their 'physicals'. If they are successful, the prospect awaits of weekends being sent to sleep in the open with no shelter and nothing to eat except what they can kill. The most successful boys spend these weekends beating up local market traders, safe in the knowledge that the officers in charge of the Army think they are part of the Navy, and vice versa. The result is that any complaint made about their behaviour will be passed endlessly back and forth between the two (who will deny ever having had responsibility for the Marines).

The Royal Signals

If you are of a gentlemanly disposition, the Signals section is for you. Not only will you find at your disposal a stereogram, leather armchairs, darts board, and well-stocked refrigerator (the contents of which are regularly deployed with devastating effect on night exercises), but you will get the chance to twiddle the knobs of your transmitter while attempting to make contact with other doughty signallers in the dark.

---

*Royal Academy.

The Marching Band

The Corps Band is the most sought-after posting. The only qualification you need to join this outfit is an ability to play a musical instrument to a moderate standard. The highlight of last year's Annual Inspection was the band's performance of 'The Grenadier Guards' arranged for thirteen triangles, a trumpet, two clarinets, two cellos, a double bass and a grand piano as Sergeant R.V.O. Parker struggled to get them to march in step.

PACK UP YOUR TROUBLES IN YOUR OLD KIT BAG

Whichever section you finally join, when you come to the end of the long afternoons of square-bashing and learning the semaphore signals for 'Simpkins is a Scrotum',* it will be time to put these hard-earned skills to test in the field. You will go on Manoeuvres.

Manoeuvres begin with a night exercise, which is spent crawling through the mud in search of 'hostile units'. These can be spotted easily because the handkerchiefs tied round their wrists are of a different colour to your own. Your job is to ambush the enemy and 'kill' them by daringly snatching their hankies. Then, when you have spent three hours hiding in a ditch and have accidentally committed suicide by blowing your nose, it'll be time to head back to the warm campfire, where you will find the schoolmasters co-ordinating the whole exercise by drinking whisky and speaking in code.

But if you think this is your cue to sit round the glowing embers smoking cigarettes, think again. While the masters in their new uniforms reminisce about the two weeks they spent at Sandhurst learning how to be CCF officers and how they narrowly avoided being called up for the Iraq war, RSM Nails really does intend to push you to the limit. Over the next three days, he wants to find out whether you have the mettle to be a Leader of Men. And he will not be satisfied until he is sure that you are capable of…

Survival

The key to survival is the kit list. Be warned: this document is really a trick to see whether you are sharp enough to spot that whoever put it together (i.e. RSM Nails) is a sadistic practical joker.

The literal-minded boy who actually packs the three mess tins, dress uniform, 1940s spyglass, table-sized map with model tanks (and wooden tank-sliders), swagger stick and all the other items into his rucksack will soon find it weighs half as much as he does. If you are this boy, your mistake will be hammered home to you on the twenty-mile route march made necessary by the RSM sleeping in the Corps minibus and running down the battery by keeping the fan heater on all night.

To pass your second survival test, you must ignore the instruction to bring your pyjamas with you. The boy who takes his pyjamas on Night Exercise always has them forcibly removed on the first night before being taken outside and dropped into the ordure pit. This in turn excludes him from the subsequent bedtime jollities, such as stuffing hay into Simpkins's mouth every time he tries to speak and the obligatory fart-lighting competition.

Initiative

Your initiative will be tested by having to ferry your kit across a stream, together with half a ton of logs and Simpkins (playing the part of a wounded soldier on a stretcher). You would find this perfectly straightforward if you had been issued with something more practical than two punctured oil drums, a plank, a washing line and a bent, metal pole. You would also find it easier if you hadn't been told that you must, on no account, leave either Simpkins or the logs unguarded on either side of the stream. To pass the test, you need to make a pontoon bridge by strapping Simpkins to the logs and getting your platoon to walk over him with the kit.

Map-reading

If you are to have a hope of passing the map-reading test, you need to cultivate the company of a boy who is born to command. When faced with the prospect of leading your platoon over twenty-five miles of hostile terrain, he will instead march you all via a circuitous route to a bus stop, hail a ride into town and escort you to a public house. You will then buy him half-pints of Cumberland Ale and, in return, he will train you in the map-reading skills required to concoct plausible reasons for why none of you met your impatient schoolmasters at the 2,000ft checkpoint.

Leadership

This is the most important test of all. When the RSM insists on a second day of forced marching, the true leader will ensure that his comrades in arms get plenty of breaks to catch their breath and rest their weary limbs. If this task falls to you, make sure to keep your knife handy so that, when your troops are flagging, you can simply cut the straps that secure Fraser's roll mat to his rucksack. The time it will take him to fetch it from the bottom of a 400ft incline should give the rest of you and your chums plenty of time to recuperate. Make the most of it: you'll need every ounce of strength when Nails finally catches up with you.

THE CHILD TURNING INTO A MAN

SWINESEND SOCIETIES

As you get older, you will discover that there are two kinds of Swinesend boy. The first keeps his nose clean, hands in his prep on time and aspires to rise through the ranks from Assistant Second Librarian until he reaches that glorious day when he dons the silver waistcoat buttons of a School Praepostor.

You are not that type of boy. Hated by the School authorities and fellow pupils alike, you will slowly begin to resent the simple pleasures of having your ribs crushed tightly between two forwards on the playing fields, or of running round the School fields in Corps uniform with the back end of a tree trunk slung over your shoulder. And when that happens, you will quickly begin to believe that the whole of School life is designed to keep you from moments of contemplation and the forbidden postcard collection you keep hidden under your mattress. You won't care less whether you win your School colours or became a Praepostor.

You may seek to conceal this fact by mooching around the House, but the pervasive odour of foetid Fifth Former and boiled cabbage, coupled with the sound of dripping taps and unearthly sounds emanating from the changing rooms, will eventually force you outside.

Luckily, the School has a number of activities on offer which will put a spring in your step in no time at all. These include:

Drama Society

There are two reasons why boys join the Drama Society: because they might get the chance either to smoke or to kiss a girl on stage. If you have any acting talent at all, Mr Jackson, the Drama teacher, will not give you a part that will allow you to do either. Instead, he is likely to decide you are perfect for the part of the Corpse in a three-hour Latvian absurdist drama translated into English by himself.

Wildlife Society

The prospect of spending an afternoon crawling through the nearby woodlands ostensibly searching for flora and fauna might seem the ideal opportunity to indulge in a few cans of cider or cigarettes. Be warned: Dr Edmonds only runs the Society because he hopes to catch boys in these nefarious activities. He is, however, afraid of spiders so if you can introduce one into the case in which he keeps his heat-sensitive binoculars you might manage to salvage something from a field trip.

The League of Nations Society
Formed in 1923, this club provides the useful service of padding the curriculum vitae of even the laziest of boys.

Dripsey Society
This intellectual fellowship is named after Swinesend's most distinguished scholar, Sir Thomas Dripsey (1823–97), who after forty years of biblical study determined that the garden of Eden had been located on the outskirts of Colwyn Bay; that the anti-Christ would probably be called Alwyn; and that because God rested on the seventh day, mankind was supposed to work only on that day to cover for His absence.

Membership is open only to Sixth Formers and is by the invitation of the Headmaster, who chairs the meetings in his study underneath the gaze of Sir Thomas's skull (acquired from the National Museum of the Philippines in 1980, where it had been deposited by a benevolent tribe of head-hunters). Members meet to discuss the fine arts and philosophy, concentrating in particular on methods to convince Oxbridge admissions tutors that you really do have an interest in these matters when you are, in fact, bluffing shamelessly.

The Spelunking Club
If your time at school has not satisfied your taste for squeezing into tight places, suffering from hypothermia or risking death from exhaustion, drowning or falling, you can get more of these by taking up caving. At present there is no master in charge of this club: Mr Bridger is still missing somewhere under Somerset after last summer's trip to Wookey Hole.

The Debating Society

One of Swinesend's oldest societies, it holds weekly, topical debates on controversial issues. It is not simply the preserve of pompous boys who want to be barristers when they grow up: all members are encouraged freely to express their views (which are then duly noted by the Head Boy and passed to the Headmaster).

The Christian Union

The CU at Swinesend is a place where you can meet, pray and practise Christianity. Members take such a literal view of their religion that they cause the Chaplain to cross the road whenever he sees them. The most bullied boys in the School, members spend their meetings praying that their tormentors see the light or else suffer an eternity of double Physics. Sadly, each year, thanks to some cruel caprice, the most attractive girl in the Lower VI always joins. She will never believe your argument that, since you were made in His image, God really does approve of your most unwholesome urges, so you'd be much wiser to drop the subject and sign up for...

The Self-Abuse Club

While you will normally be able to contain your urges with a fulfilling tussle on the playing fields, you may sometimes find yourself tempted to indulge in acts of beastliness. Fortunately, as an imaginative boy, reared on tales of Juvenal, Aristophanes and Petronius, you may transcend wickedness by joining the Self-Abuse Club.

The Club has long been the most popular in the School and has had an ever-growing number of members since it was first founded in 1856. The traditional single-handed game is still regularly played, but the Club is also home to a number of unusual and team-building variants, all of which are guaranteed to ensure a prodigious ordering of your senses and, in many instances, clear up your spots:

Uppingham Doors

To most people a door is a big wooden thing with hinges and a handle;

but to the public schoolboy a door is a hotter prospect than a young Helen Mirren in a bathtub of asses' milk. To play Uppingham Doors, a game invented by Stephen Fry at that school, all you have to do is get yourself signed off Games, wait until your Boarding House is empty and then cavort naked from room to room, trapping a prominent part of your anatomy between every door and jamb you encounter along the way *without getting caught by Matron*. If she does catch you, be warned: she is likely to slam that door just a little too hard.

The Quick Dash

This variant is the most physically demanding played by Club members, and should only be attempted by those in the Third XV or better. You should first stand at the top of the stairs in your Boarding House and emit a blood-curdling scream, ending in a whimpering yelp of 'Matron'. Then dash back to your dorm and see if you can bring yourself to climax before she appears. If your trousers are still at half-mast when the dormitory door opens, this form of the game is not for you.

Tossing the Javelin

Infrequent players of the game, who have the stamina and resources to devote to it, often excel at this version. You can have as many participants as you like and the aim is shoot your beastly substance further than anyone else, rather in the manner of javelin throwing or shot-putting. However, unlike in these sports, taking a 'run-up' before 'lift-off' is forbidden.

The Biscuit Game

The classic game, beloved of all public schoolboys, was raised to an art form by generations of Swinesians. It has now attained a Zen-like quality. You stand around a digestive. The first boy to suffer from unwholesome thoughts has to take the biscuit under a cold shower and chant until the moment it dissolves. Members of the Self-Abuse club are banned from playing the Eton version of the game, which, however hard to swallow, is quite simply disgusting.

Liver

To some, uncooked offal may be the sort of thing the cat would reject with disdain. To the public school man, it offers the chthonic thrill of nature at its most untrammelled, the most primal sensual excitement, a frisson of transgression and the added bonus of showing off your knowledge of modern American literature. Especially when you've two moist pieces in a jam jar.

This game is played throughout the School and explains the almost universal unpopularity of liver at lunchtime.

FORBIDDEN PLEASURES

The Self-Abuse Club is not officially sanctioned by the authorities. However, the sense of camaraderie and shared contempt for petty regulations that it engenders make it one of the most desirable of all school activities. But overindulgence can make you weak so, when you, Byles and Bayliss are worn out by your exertions, remember that there are many other forbidden pleasures that will help you to keep your pecker up.

SMOKING

Recent changes to the law have meant that masters are no longer able to smoke in their Common Room and, because they are reluctant to risk exposure to their pupils at break time by smoking a restorative Camel in the open air, they have taken extra steps to ensure that boys cannot enjoy that which is denied to them.

Consequently, the physical and mental benefits you will gain from staying one step ahead of the irritable and nicotine-starved teachers will be incalculable. Those in doubt how to proceed need simply follow the instructions overleaf.

How to smoke

1. Assemble some like-minded chums. This should not be a
    solitary vice.

2. Locate a safe place to smoke. Time spent in reconnaissance is never
    wasted. Sometimes, the least obvious places are the most
    conspicuous: many Swinesians like to smoke openly in the High
    Street. Others have found the local park near the gentlemen's
    lavatory a better location: any master who sees you there will not
    wish it to be known that he was in the area.

3. Using your favourite method (e.g. drawing lots, choosing the oldest-
    looking boy, selecting the weediest boy who has no alternative), pick
    a boy to visit the tobacconist.

4. Tell the boy which brand you require. For the novice, a brand such
    as Player's Navy Cut will provide a smooth introduction. Low-tar
    and menthol cigarettes are suitable only for girls, while Gauloises
    either avec or sans filtre are touched only by ponces and sodomites.
    Intelligent, well-dressed Sixth Formers may, however, get away with
    a Sobranie or a Sweet Afton. Rolling tobacco is always acceptable
    and, incidentally, one can store an astonishing
    amount in the lining of one's blazer.

5. When the cigarettes or tobacco
    have been bought, send someone
    back to buy the matches,
    which will have
    been forgotten.

6. Take the stash to your
    location (see step 2).

7. Light a cigarette.

8. Choke violently and adopt
    one of the poses shown in the illustration.

DRINKING

If you develop a lasting interest in cigarette smoking, you will often find it hard to raise the money to buy fags. Fortunately, if you are an enterprising boy, there is one thing that will enable you to supplement your income with enough cash to support not only your own nicotine habit, but also that of at least three other chums. It is called 'Drink'.

Alcohol is, at Swinesend, a far more valuable form of tender than cash: it buys you popularity, influence or food that is actually digestible. And as the nearest off-licence is several miles away, it's a good idea to learn how to make it. That way, if you see a boy wandering around who has a glazed look on his face and is unable to speak, you can recruit him as a potential customer who would be only too grateful to have you supply him with some top-class hooch. (Of course, it is possible he has just escaped from a double German class with Herr Teufels, in which case the above is even more true.)

If you do start to make and sell your own alcohol, just make sure you don't make the same mistake as the Fellsgarth boy who started a fire in his Boarding House a few years ago. The subsequent investigation by the fire fighters (gleefully followed by local TV crews) led to the loss of his still, the closure of the Sixth Form drinking club (and the confiscation of its extensive archive of grade A pornographic materials). He also made an untimely appearance before the local magistrates.

Do not let this deter you, however. If you don't speculate, you won't accumulate: just make sure you know how to...

How to make moonshine

1. Pick your ingredients

If you are wise, you will confine production to vodka, as that spirit leaves no tell-tale smell on the breath. The ingredients are also easy to obtain and you will need approximately 2.5kg of sugar (or equivalent yield from potatoes) and 30g of yeast for every 10 litres of water. The House kitchen should provide all the materials you need.

2. Check your equipment

You will need a vessel in which to brew the ingredients. A milk churn or similar container from the kitchen should suffice.

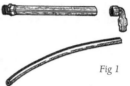

Fig 1

You will also need to raid the workshops and laboratories for lengths of copper piping and rubber tubing to make the condenser (figure 1). Some metalworking skills

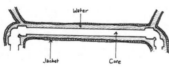

Fig 2

are needed for this. The vapours from the base will rise into the inner piping. The water that flows around the outer piping (figure 2), will help these vapours condense into spirits.

3. Fill the still

A little technical ingenuity will be required to do this. First place the ingredients in the base, then fix the condenser to the base and seal it tightly. Masking tape alone will prove inadequate, so use a punctured football (or similar) instead. Fix firmly into place.

4. Find a place to make your moonshine

You will need a constant source of heat to boil the ingredients and a constant supply of water circulating round the pipes. Look for a disused attic where there are pipes hot enough to boil the water. Even better, tap into the gas supply and use several Bunsen burners. Assuming this cannot be done, simply find any remote spot (attic, Fives court or outhouse) where you can start a fire in peace.

5. Make the moonshine

Boil the ingredients steadily but not quickly. Ensure that a couple of juniors equipped with water pistols or a foot pump keep the water flowing around the condenser. In time, the vapours will cool and condensed liquid will come out of the end of the pipe. Collect this liquid in some old lemonade bottles (see figure 3).

6. Drink it

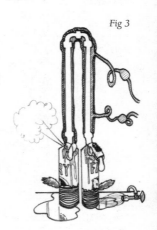

Fig 3

The first few drops may be of somewhat poor quality. Give them to your Tasting Fag to check the quality. If he goes blind, discard the liquid and start again.

Once you are satisfied, simply add the mixer of your choice and sit back to enjoy. So long as you have remembered to give the Praes their share, you will soon ensure that you never run out of cigarettes again. Indeed, you might even have some money left over to spend on...

DRUGS

For generations, boys have avoided the dangers of illegal substances by making use of substitutes. These have all the glamour associated with narcotics with few of the unpleasant side-effects (such as expulsion, a period at an expensive crammer and a job in the City). Overleaf is an at-a-glance guide to the most common legal substitutes you are likely to encounter.

Substance	Method of ingestion	Coolness quotient	High (compared with that given by 0.5g of cocaine)	
DRIED BANANA SKIN	Smoked in a spliff	4/10	0	
NUTMEG	Orally	1/10	0.01	
PRO-PLUS TABLETS	Orally	2/10	0.2	
TALCUM POWDER	Snorted	10/10	100	
TUNES	Orally	0/10	0	

Danger of overdose	Cool things to say after consumption
LOW It contains no psychoactive ingredients	'Do you know that Donovan's seminal hit "Mellow Yellow" was written under the influence of banana skins, man?'
MEDIUM (unless consumed on school rice pudding or in doses of 5–15g or more). Myristicin, a naturally occurring methylenedioxyphenyl compound found in nutmeg, causes symptoms similar to atropine poisoning when 5–15g of the spice are consumed. Symptoms include flushing of skin, tachycardia, absence of salivation, and excitation of the central nervous system	'This is seriously bad shit.'
MEDIUM The active ingredient is caffeine anhydrous Ph. Eur. (of which each tablet contains 50mg). Side-effects of an overdose include stomach pain; anxiety; confusion or delirium; convulsions; dehydration; tachycardia; fever; frequent urination; headache; irritability; twitching; nausea and vomiting; ringing or other sounds in ears; seeing flashes of light; trouble in sleeping	'Because these pills are made by Bayer Health Care I always use them responsibly and in accordance with the manufacturer's instructions' or 'Christ! I feel totally wired.'
LOW 0.5g contains only slightly less cocaine than 0.5g of cocaine purchased from your local dealer	'What is that cloying scent of lily of the valley?'
HIGH Active ingredients are menthol and sugar. Effects of prolonged use may include rapid formation of dental caries and cavities	'Hmm. I can breathe more easily.'

STRANGE STIRRINGS

Is that a *GIRL* I see before me?

One day you will experience a moment when even the pleasures of drink and drugs pall. It happens when you walk into a classroom and realize that something is badly wrong. At first you will assume that the blonde, long-haired creature beside you is Simpkins with a more than usually idiotic simper on his face. Then it will hit you. You are in the Sixth Form and girls are now allowed to share your lessons.

When you find yourself in the same room as a girl, stay calm. Remember that the days when the groundsman would chase girls off the premises and you could get expelled for saying 'good morning' to your sister are now long gone. Nowadays the School trusts you to treat girls as equals, or at least people with parents who pay equal fees: you'll have to overcome this challenge by yourself.

The second thing to do is to make sure that the person you are looking at really is a girl. A degree of terror and mistrust is quite natural but, before you flee the room and seek sanctuary, it's as well to make sure that you are not running away from an upended mop that someone has left in the corner of the room.

To help you avoid doing this, we have put together a simple table that will help you decide what to do next:

What do I do with this girl, sir?

Most boys have mothers. The more observant ones will notice that there is something different about them. It is only a foolish boy, however, who thinks that the fragrant lady who stifled a sob as she left him at the door of his House three or four years ago is typical of womankind. She is not.

It is no surprise, then, that when you first come face-to-face with an authentic girl in the Sixth Form you will feel threatened by her superior academic ability, greater maturity and effortless talent for bedazzling your chums.

What is even worse, each time you attempt to further Simpkins's education by sticking a Bunsen burner up his nose, you will hear her tut-tutting at the back of the laboratory before one of her chums dares her to alert the authorities to your transgression. After your fourth detention, you may well start harbouring a grudge against this female menace.

Then, as you finish your lines, the truth will dawn on you: *she admires you*. She couldn't care less whether you pull Baker's chair from under him as he sits down, she just wishes that you would pay her a bit more attention. This can be tricky but with a little effort can be achieved with only a little embarrassment to all concerned:

1. Don't go by appearances

As she walked for the first time with the new girls into Chapel, you and the other judges will, as is traditional, have awarded them marks out of ten for appearance, demeanour and breast size. She may now mutter about 'puerile, sexist behaviour', but she will actually be rather flattered that you voted her 'best of the rest' after Jocasta Wadebridge.

2. Play hard to get

By all means make a good impression, but don't be too eager. If you are, you will spend the next couple of years listening to the object of your affections say that you're *just good friends*.

This is what happened to Simpkins when Janet Hamilton-Bayley correctly deduced that his simpering was simply an attempt to cover up the fact he was mentally explaining to her the offside rule in football. She made him her satchel carrier and subsequently learnt, much to the delight of everyone she told, of his fear that a fencing injury had left him unable to fully taste a woman's love.

To avoid this fate, you should simply treat all girls from the outset with icy detachment: if one speaks to you, say nothing and imagine that the space she is occupying is no more threatening than a few cubic feet of fresh air.

3. Then warm to your theme

Eventually, you may feel sufficiently intimate with a female to call her by her surname. Deploy this technique carefully. To avoid the appearance of being over-eager (see above) it is best to leave your chosen girl with the sensation that you had no choice but to speak to her. For example, if asking her to lend you a pencil, it's best to borrow the technique perfected by Byles Major, who, in this situation, tends to blush, stutter and run his hands through his hair a few times. Considerate as ever, he always returns the girl's pencil wordlessly, and always when she's not looking.

4. GSOH required

Above all else, girls like a boy who can make them laugh. So, to win the affection of a girl, you can't beat breaking into her House and hiding there till nightfall. That way you can raise merry giggles by jumping out of wardrobes in the middle of the night, putting cling-film over the lavatories, scattering 'difficult-to-deny-convincingly' items of underclothing in their rooms and hiding any hairbrushes or make-up bags you come across (giving you extra fun the next morning as you look for the girl who has been dealt the most bruises by her chums). They love it!

Manners maketh man

Legend has it that an Etonian, a Wykehamist and a Harrovian were all competing for the favours of a stunningly beautiful girl. The Etonian noticed she had no chair, the Wykehamist brought her one and the Harrovian sat on it.
But what would you do in response to the same situation?

1. Suggest the girl fetch herself a chair.
2. Studiously ignore her and study the ceiling instead.
3. Fetch two chairs.
4. Tell her to fetch two chairs.
5. Invite her to sit on your lap.
6. Tell her to sit on the floor and stop complaining.*

---

*Answer: Appealing as option 5, is, this will expose you to significant discomfort after five or so minutes. If you have any regard for your own comfort the answer will be 4. Tell her to fetch two chairs. Ordering her about will, in any case, provide her with a secret thrill, provided you do it in a sufficiently masterful fashion. If you can't manage this, then just what *have* you been doing at school?

LIGHTS, GYMSLIPS, ACTION!

You would be a most unusual public school boy if you did not believe that all girls are desperate to go out with you. You would be even more remarkable if you let evidence to the contrary deflect you.

Imagine, for instance, that you have convinced a girl to let you escort her back to her Boarding House late at night. The moon shines brightly, there is a warm breeze, the nightingales chip in with a bit of romantic warbling and the night air carries the distant sound of the local chavs treating your schoolmates to a spot of GBH. But what's this the girl is saying in curt tones? That she's got a headache and a boyfriend back home?

The worst thing you can do in such a situation is to take such a confession lying down. It's a challenge, after all, so keep on giving her a good dose of attention whether she says she wants it or not.

There is no better way of doing this than to join the Film Club and offer her the part as the leading lady in a movie. Boys who have made a careful study of Scandinavian and Japanese art-house flicks available from the library in the boiler room of Cockchafer's should have developed a suitable appreciation of the art to make bold statements such as this.

Boys with an especially strong creative urge may wish to produce a short film of their own. The tools and materials that you will need to make a small masterpiece are commonplace and easily obtained.

You will need:
- One dormitory with a cupboard
- One drill (optional)
- One bed (minimum)
- At least one girlfriend (ideally blonde)
- One or more rugby players

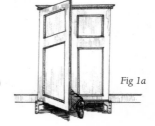

Fig 1a

- A battery-powered film or digital camera
- Champagne
- Oysters

Fig 1b

Method

Ensure that you are alone in the dormitory and, if possible, lock the door. Stand inside the cupboard (Fig. 1a) and ensure that you have an unimpeded view of the bed (Fig. 1b).

Fig 2a

Get out of the cupboard and test that the battery in your camera (Fig. 2a) is fully charged. Having done this, place the camera on a cupboard shelf (Fig. 2b).

If you are confident that you will not be overheard, carefully use a ⅛" drill bit to bore a clean hole in the cupboard door, exactly opposite the centre of the camera lens. You will end up with poorly defined images if the hole is any smaller.

Fig 2b

Fig 2c

When you are satisfied that the camera is sufficiently concealed and in satisfactory working order, you are ready for filming. Unlock the door (Fig. 2c).

You will now need your girlfriend. Invite her to sit on the bed and suggest some 'full-on stuff', possibly involving the champagne (Fig. 3) and oysters (Fig. 4).

Fig 3

When you have finished, see your girlfriend safely out of the dorm and circulate copies of the film you have

Fig 4

just made amongst all the boys in the Sixth Form Common Room. Not only will your actions win you nationwide fame, but you can be sure that your girlfriend will not forget you in a hurry and may even invite you to meet her father, three brothers and slightly sinister uncle.

COMMENT IS FREE

PUBLISH AND BE TANNED

If you can't make your name in such a way, you may well find yourself on the cusp of the Upper VI without having made your mark on the School. But if your overuse of artificial stimulants has left you dazed and unable to shine on the playing field, the hookah pipe in your study has failed to attract you the notoriety you deserve and your undying love continues to be spurned by Jocasta Wadebridge, there is still one avenue open to you.

For more than two centuries, young Swines have settled their reckoning with a callous and ungrateful School by producing publications with witty titles such as *The Porker*, *The Truffler* and *Private Sty*.

In the past you had to rely on outside printers to produce your magazine, which you would then distribute around the Boarding Houses at the dead of night. School-wide notoriety would invariably follow when the magazine was suppressed after three editions because the printer had rung up the Headmaster to ask whether he was sure that the answers to the wordsearch puzzle shouldn't actually read 'Jenkins is a runt' and 'Mr Stockwell sucks bricks'.

Those days are now gone and, today, technology makes it much easier: you can simply set up a website instead. While boys at other institutions make do with a scurrilous blog or page on MySpace or Bebo, at Swinesend we are far more sophisticated: Minns Minor of VC has installed a server in the old boiler room under St Leger's House, where he rents rack space from the House Captain and allows you to set up a site with its own domain name. Of course, if you are to win fame as a budding satirist by being denounced and hauled before the Headmaster, you must leave tracks to ensure that the School's computer technicians can prove you've used their equipment to set up a popular school site like:

www.hotpork.com
Established by some enterprising members of Cockchafer's Lower VI, this site allows you to rate the School's girls in various artistic poses. It has delighted the popular press and dismayed the Board of Governors, which has asked Geography Master Mr Wilson to take leave of absence while the police investigate the allegation that he has downloaded seventy-three indecent images of Jocasta Wadebridge with her younger sister, Lolita.

www.feebay.com
Secret information on all the country's top public schools can be yours at a price. A group of enterprising hackers in the Lower VI has acquired information on what next year's fees will be, which schools are under investigation by the DTI, how many masters have been forced to take extended leave of absence and the number of scurvy cases in each dormitory. This information has given rise to many a lucrative bidding war between newspapers and the school authorities.

www.swinebet.com
One of the Economics Sixth's 'side-projects', this site was founded to make Sports Day betting as simple as possible. The site's undoing was its decision to offer markets on other aspects of School life (such as the number of pregnancies each term and how many times the Chaplain

was found 'resting' in the cricket pavilion). After the Head of
Economics, Dr Trowbridge, 'bought' heavily on the number of
suspensions he would hand out each term, he rusticated his entire
class, which is now unable to return to school until they raise the
money for his winnings.

www.swotornot.com
Widely blamed for the School's plummeting GCSE results, this site
gives you the chance to rate your classmates' swottiness on a scale of 1
to 10. Saddleworth Minor, who gained an average rating of 10 (from
4,967 votes), was voted the undisputed swot of the Lower IV until he
hanged himself from the Art Shack rafters last term.

REPORTS

If you take to online journalism too enthusiastically, you will find that
your schoolmasters include what they believe is hard-hitting prose in
your end-of-term report. But don't worry, when you hear your father
read it to you, you will certainly be at a loss to understand how the
remarks made by your teachers bear any relation to what actually
happened in the preceding three months. This is because, at
Swinesend, reports are written in the shorthand which has served the
School well for decades. They convey the impression that you have
made on the staff more succinctly and accurately than the detailed
profiles that have now become fashionable at other schools.

To unlock the meaning of your report, all you need do is consult the
table overleaf.

Only the Headmaster departs from this formula. This is rare but he
sometimes extemporizes should he recall a particularly comedic
performance in the School Play or a brave tackle on the football pitch.
These comments should not worry you (even if you have never been in
the School Play or played football for your House): they are invariably
illegible.

Report	Meaning
Excellent!	This boy is quite good at [*insert subject*].
A good term's work.	I recall this boy.
A fair term's work.	I do not recall this boy.
Shows promise.	I have conceived an unhealthy attachment to this boy and will be looking for ways to spend time 'mentoring' him in future.
Must try harder.	If he ever submitted his prep I might have some idea as to his abilities.
A disruptive influence.	He is clever and funny. This cannot be tolerated.
Quite the stupidest boy I have ever taught.	He will probably go on to great things and this is the best way I have of making sure he remembers me.
Trying.	He *is* the stupidest boy I have ever taught.
Very trying.	I like to think of myself as a comedian.
I predict a bright future.	Because his parents will buy him one.
Quite stupendously dull. He needs to get a grip.	His attempt to be clever by submitting his first Ancient History essay in Latin has failed to impress because I do not welcome the extra work.
He will never amount to much.	And will probably become a teacher so I had better make sure it's not in this subject.

Speech Day

If your parents confined themselves to reading your school reports, and never set foot near the School, your quality of life would be greatly improved. Unfortunately, Speech Day at Swinesend occurs on the last day of Trinity term and it will confirm what you will have long suspected: yours are the world's most embarrassing parents.

Their car, their clothes, their accents, the way they greet you, the way they talk about you to your teachers, other parents and your chums all contrive to make an already insufferable day excruciating. It is not just their insistence on calling you by the pet name you had when you were a toddler, or their continual mention of the promise you showed when they enrolled you in a pre-school ballet class: it is their invariable habit of referring to you in the third person even when you are standing right in front of them.

Indeed, so embarrassing are your parents that even sitting through Taylor collecting his third prize of the afternoon and watching the Junior Gym Squad perform physical jerks provides an almost welcome respite from the horror. You will, however, be brought back to their true awfulness when they stand and cheer wildly as you trudge up to receive the Upper IV Cup for Most Improved Boy.

But there is one thing you can do to take your mind off this humiliation. One small solace you can take. You can watch the spectacle of one fidgeting and glassy-eyed group enjoying the occasion almost as little as you do: the masters. For them each moment listening to speeches is time in the pub lost.

A moment's reflection will reveal the real purpose of Speech Day. This event takes place not only to humiliate you by bringing home to you that your parents really do exist, it is also the occasion when the Headmaster metes out a collective punishment to his staff: the more numerous their year's transgressions, the more tedious his own speech and the longer he keeps them from the revivifyng tinctures which they crave on this last day of the School Year.

In a good year he may limit himself to listing those to whom the School owes a particular debt of gratitude (starting with the Chairman of the Governors and finishing with the Under-Groundsman). If he is particularly displeased, he will prolong the agony by giving a match-by-match account of the First XV's now forgotten winter season which resulted in a well-deserved place in the quarter-finals of the Public Schools Championship (the best result for fifteen years).

This is bad enough, but there is always worse to come: after the Latin Speech, the Headmaster introduces the Guest Speaker – whom he has selected with care to reflect how poorly his staff has behaved during the year. If the year's only misdemeanour has been the Art Master parking in the Headmaster's space or getting drunk at his wife's Christmas sherry party, the Head may introduce a bluff military gentleman who confines his remarks to one anecdote about his time in Burma and an exhortation for boys to Play the Game.

On the other hand, if things have gone particularly badly and the Head has been run out in the Masters v Boys cricket match, it is a racing certainty that he will welcome Mr Justice Dudley who was at *this very school* sixty years previously, or the local MP, Mr Kevin Ufford, who will give the same soul-shattering speech he did on his last three visits.

So, as your father swerves out alarmingly onto the bypass and your trunk rattles around in the back of the ancient parental Volvo, you can start the ten weeks of glorious summer vacation with a prayer that it will prove long enough for all your friends to forget you are in any way related or connected to these frightful people. And, as you travel further and further from the School grounds, you can indeed reflect on the truth of the maxim uttered by every schoolmaster as they put the whole of Upper IV in detention for the misdemeanours of one boy: *Life is indeed unfair.*

OLD SWINESIANS

How to avoid the Old Boys' Association

It might seem unimaginable to you now, but in five years' time you will have sat through your last ever Speech Day. The Headmaster will have given you his traditional leaving advice to avoid fornication. You'll have received an indifferent set of A-Level results and got blisteringly drunk on the town meadows. You might even have shaved off Simpkins's eyebrows as a leaving present. But the time will have come for you to leave Swinesend and make your way in the world. As you leave, you will be given an invitation to join the Old Swinesians' Association.

Naturally you will have no desire to join. Five years in the company of Simpkins, Bayliss, Byles *et al.* are more than enough. Once you leave school, the fabled insolent charm, singular attitude towards women and damn-you swagger which are known and admired as the hallmarks of a Swinesend man will be enough to keep you in spiritual contact with your roots.

The danger, though, comes in early middle age. It is then that Swinesians can fall into the trap of behaving like the sort of Old Boy who actually does attend Old Boys' events. In some cases, they do this because they were viciously bullied at school and now wish to brag about their successful careers to their tormentors; in others because they simply cannot remember their time at school. Men like these invariably spend years attending functions at which they are always reduced to approaching ruddy-faced ex-schoolmasters and saying, 'Are you sure you don't remember me, sir?'

You will realize it is much kinder on your chums and your former teachers to let them go through life remembering you as you were when you left school for the last time, a cigarette dangling from your lips and the School crest half ripped from your blazer pocket. The only failsafe way of doing this is to outwit the secretary of the Old Swinesians' Association at every turn and prevent him from tracking you down. You can do this by taking the following precautions:

1. Move house every six months
And always register the utility bills under an alias or in your wife's maiden name.

2. Fake your own death
Leave your clothes on a lonely beach at high tide and take care to leave some personal identification in the jacket pocket. Make sure this includes a will in which you leave all your possessions (a couple of paperback Buchan novels, a half-empty bottle of whisky and a pile of unpaid bills) to Swinesend. You could also arrange for an accomplice to discover your body and register the death, but there's always the risk he will blackmail you with threats to grass you up to the OS Association.

3. Undergo plastic surgery
Quite the best way to avoid recognition by fellow Old Swines who might let slip your whereabouts. Just make sure you don't end up with the face of someone who went to a different school, otherwise you'll end up avoiding two Old Boys' clubs.

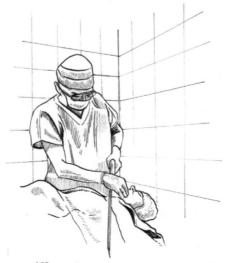

4. Hire a *Doppelgänger*

If you can afford to hire a lookalike, simply register his address with the Association and he can deal with the endless begging letters and attend the Old Boys' functions on your behalf.

5. Choose your career carefully

Under no circumstances join a profession that has a register of any kind, such as the Church, Medicine or the Bar. Avoid also any career that will attract you unwelcome publicity: every newspaper report will gleefully refer to your educational background (and if you are really unfortunate, you may end up being invited to join the flourishing branch of the OS Association at Ford Open Prison).

Ideally, you should become a spy, which would also allow you to employ your counter-espionage skills to outfox the Old Swinesians' Association; but if you're not good enough to join the Secret Services, you can always be a journalist. That way, you can write under the pen name of 'Simpkins' and, should you be unmasked, you could publish an article in a national newspaper in which you magnify every trifling indignity you suffered during your time at Swinesend into a gross breach of your human rights. They won't touch you after reading that.

6. Avoid places where other Old Swines are likely to gather

Apart from avoiding the obvious sorts of places (chambers of commerce, Pioneer Corps messes, recreational houses of correction near the Inns of Court, etc.), it's probably wise to move somewhere you would never expect to find an Old Swine. While it might not be necessary to go into hiding and grow a beard, doing the equivalent – e.g. opening a health food shop on a council estate in Glasgow or devoting your life to intellectual pursuits – might be advisable.

7. Disgrace yourself

The OS Association Rules state that members found guilty of excessive whore-mongering, fraud, misuse of the OS colours, defacing the Founder's Statue or membership of subversive organizations can be struck from the records. Ideally, you will commit one of the above offences while wearing your OS tie. Be warned, however, that any or all of the above offences may be cancelled out if you become a war hero, or so famous that the School decides to claim the credit for you: if this happens, you will probably be made an Honorary Life Member and forced to attend the annual dinner.

The biggest danger of letting the Old Swinesians' Association catch up with you, however, is the fact that it will never, ever give you the space and time needed to let your mental scars heal – even if you live on the other side of the world. It achieves this by attempting to send you a copy of the School magazine at the end of every summer term. Your parents will be sent a copy before you arrive at the School, so if you read it, you'll see what we mean.

Swines!

(formerly *The Swinesian*)

Whitsun Term, 2007

FROM THE HEADMASTER

The past year has once again been one of the most
historic I can remember. Although the School
sometimes appears to be changing at a bewildering
pace, I am confident that even the most traditionally
minded Swinesian will agree that much of it has been
for the better.

Last year, for the first time ever, the School raised
an equal amount of money from the parents of girls as
it did from the parents of boys. While this is an
important milestone, it does not, of course, mean
that we now allow the girls to 'take over the place'
(as the Bursar delicately put it.) We are ploughing
the additional income into extra security for the
girls' Boarding Houses, regrettably necessary after
last year's 'headless man' incident.

On a related note, I am delighted to report that Mr
Spofforth's operation was completely successful and
that he will be rejoining the staff this term as Miss
Spofforth. PE lessons will never be the same again!

A much more contentious change was the decision to
abolish the Sambo Day celebrations. I appreciate that
many, if not most of you, had fond memories of this
ancient custom and I have received many letters on
the subject: 'There was certainly nothing racist
about the mock lynching,' wrote one of you. 'I
remember blacking up for the ceremony myself in 1950.
When I joined the Rhodesian police force, it gave me,
if anything, a greater sympathy for the plight of the
native population.'

But times change and, after a probe by the Commission for Racial Equality, we have regretfully decided to dispense with the services of Mr 'Chokey' Aderounmu, our gifted banjo teacher, in anticipation of the drop in demand.

Next year the event will be replaced by 'Diversity Awareness Day' and boys will work with members of the Swinesend Association for the Advancement of Coloured People to encourage members of local ethnic communities to take part in specially designed workshops on 'Swinesend Values and Culture'. We are delighted that we have been awarded a substantial Home Office grant to carry out this work, especially as we could no longer afford to fight the local constabulary's decision to prosecute the entire Lower IV for inciting racial hatred during last year's performance of 'Hold Them Down, You Zulu Warriors' ('High Zigga Zoomba') in the market square.

There is, of course, more that we can do and, perhaps, in future the authorities will give a more fitting recognition to our efforts to help the community at large. I am delighted to announce that, as of next year, thanks to a generous subsidy, we will now let pupils from Swinesend Community College use the swimming pool for thirty minutes on every alternate Monday morning. I must appeal to you all for understanding, and trust that you will be able to endure the stench of the extra disinfectant we will be using. Remember, always, that it is for the Good of the School.

Floreat Swinesendia!

Tim Taylor, CBE, B.Ed.

CLUBS AND SOCIETIES

LOWER VI ART SOCIETY

Members of the Lower VI art club staged a very successful art exhibition at the Swinesend Arts Centre, which was opened by old boy Dickie Adcock, the well-known Leicestershire watercolourist. The theme of the exhibition was 'Young British Swines' and boys presented works in a variety of media that, for them, were a visual metaphor of their time at the School. Star of the show was J. B. Embon's *Everyone I Have Wanted to Shoot in the Head 2002–2006*, a Corps tent embroidered with the names of boys and masters whose lives the artist has dreamed of terminating.

The exhibition as a whole was highly successful and received a very positive write-up in the *Swinesend Trumpet*, which declared it 'so frightening it makes one question what the School – and our beautiful town – is nurturing in its bosom'.

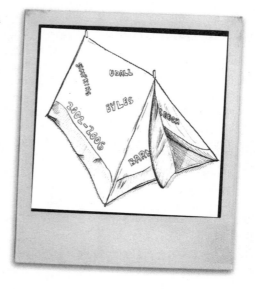

For those who were unable to attend the exhibition, we hope the pictures of selected artworks will go at least a little way to making up for it.

'I was inspired by Marc Quinn's "Self", which was a cast of his own head made out of his own blood," explains Carr. "I was a bit short of time, though. So I thought I'd use Watkins Minor's blood to make a model of his head – with his head still in it. And the great thing is, I don't have to worry about switching the freezer off by mistake.'

'Other' by D. S. Carr.

'Some people have claimed that I pinched the idea. Not so. I simply killed the Headmaster's cat and wanted to find a way to keep on looking at the body.'

'The Physical Impossibility of Pussy in the Mind of a Boy at Swinesend' by T. W. Atkins

THE FOLK CLUB

Whilst the traditional element remains strong in this club – thanks to lifelong Dylan fan Mr Bergin, who founded and still runs it – even he was forced to concede that there was something something else blowin' in the wind at the club's annual concert in the Memorial Hall. Mr Bergin opened proceedings with a selection of his own ballads about sewage workers during the Great Depression and was met with a typically appreciative shower of bottles. However, it was clear that most in the crowd were really waiting for the School's hottest new acts.

The most credible boys in this society have always found a way to express their uniquely misunderstood character by fitting in with the other band members. This year discerning boys agree that, thanks to his chronic lack of self-confidence, clinical depression, unhealthy fascination with the Third Reich and early death, Joy Division singer Ian Curtis is the ideal role model.

After assuring their ascendancy by beating up the Fourth Formers who turned up wearing Slipknot merchandise, arranging for the constabulary to bust the Pete Doherty wannabes and locking the School's single Nick Drake fan inside the music room, the Curtis enthusiasts were ready to take the stage.

Recently renamed boy band New Boarder's combination of *a capella* cover versions of Curtis's songs and snappy dance routines won them a large following in the girls' Houses and sections of the Common Room, but the real stars were Goy Division. Their set, which fused Manchester post-punk with Klezmer, was met with the ultimate accolade – studied indifference.

HISTORY SOCIETY

The once moribund History Society is one of the liveliest clubs in the School now that it is run by Mr Irving Springett, the enthusiastic young History Master. Mr Springett has encouraged a controversial approach to local history and seeks to correct many of the commonly accepted beliefs about the School. Last term he caused a furore when he invited Mr Peter Bexley, the revisionist historian, to present a paper that refuted the view of the local archaeological society that the stones used to build the new Common Room came from a Roman bath house. Bexley insisted instead that newly discovered documents proved that the stones came, in fact, from a Victorian larder. This hypocaust denial is now the subject of court proceedings.

IN BRIEF

1. The Philosophy Club has been disbanded, much to the outrage of former members who contend that it never existed in the first place.

2. G. O. Higgs, captain of the Swinesend Athletics Society, is appealing for the return of the club hurdles. For the time being, they are using junior boys to jump over, but find the fact that their height is not adjustable a considerable disadvantage.

3. The Evangelical Society had a good response to its African Famine Appeal and will be able to send 100 copies of the Book of Common Prayer to succour those troubled by imminent starvation. Thanks to all who contributed.

4. Swinesend's Friends of Zimbabwe group is now the proud owner of 10,000 acres of farm land (formerly the property of Col. Jock Calverton). Members are now trying to work out how to farm them!

CLASSICS IS FUN Really?!

Whoever said you'd never need Classics once you've left school? Surely they haven't forgotten the annual Latin and Greek prize. This fun competition, open to all Swinesians past and present, is simply irresistible.

THIS YEAR'S PRIZES

1st Prize: A £100 voucher redeemable at the School Shop
2nd Prize: Tickets for the annual First XI vs Kettering Cricket Club fixture.
3rd Prize: Signed calendar featuring the School's Top Choristers.

Part 1
I. Render the following speech of the Rt Hon. John Prescott MP into Latin prose in the style of Cicero

'It is a fact that homelessness has continued to rise. It doubled under the previous Administration, but that does not help us. The Government intend to reduce – and probably eliminate – the homeless by 2008. [Interruption.] I am sorry, but the House knows that I have problems with English. I did not go to public school, so there is a limit to what I am able to say. Opposition Members can be such twits. We believe that we can eliminate the problem of homelessness by providing more resources, which is precisely what we are doing.'*

II. Render the following passage from Mr Prescott into Latin hexameters (after the manner of Vergil)

'I have made my mistakes. I have made my denials. But I will keep on going with my job. People must judge me with what I do on the job.'

*House of Commons *Hansard*, 2004-07-13, Column 1268.

Part 2

Translate the following gobbets into Greek

1. Ancilla, quae Psyche vocabatur, lodiculam in pavimento diligenter extendit. Sollicitavit inguina mea mille iam mortibus frigida (Petronius, *Satyricon* XX)

2. nam a prima statim pueritia turpis, improbus, crudelis, libidinosus, ore quoque pollutus et constupratus fuit (*Scriptores Historiae Augustae*, Comm. I.7)

3. Heiroclem vero sic amavit ut eidem inguina oscularetur (*Scriptores Historiae Augustae*, Elag. VI.5)

4. ita fustibus sum mollior magis quam ullus cinaedus (Plautus, *Aulularia* 42)

All entries to reach Dr Meredith, Head of Classics, by 1 September. We regret that we cannot enter into any correspondence.

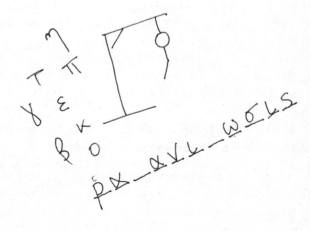

9

SCHOOL LIFE

'You should take an intelligent interest in the School, boy!'

On almost every occasion I have seen him over the last three years, Mr Panton has given me this singularly well-considered piece of advice. I was unable to act on it as all my spare time has been spent reconstructing a scale model of the Croatian state railway system on the Upper Waste. But now that's finished, I've finally decided to act on it.

Dear reader, **did you know…**?

1. The combined weight of the Upper V (term beginning): **970 stones**
2. The combined weight of the Upper V (term end): **824½ stones**
3. The decline in the instances of botulism over the past three years: **17%**
4. The number of desks in the whole school: **754**
5. The average number of graffito items on a school desk: **16.7645**
6. The total increase in school fees over the past three years: **45.65%**
7. School fees as a percentage of the National Average Wage: **73%**
8. School groundsman's salary as a percentage of the National Average Wage: **62.58%**
9. The average age of an Upper V text book: **17.3 years**
10. The average number of exercise books per boy marked termly by Mr George, the Maths Master: **0.1134**
11. The number of times this term the Chaplain has been unable to officiate at morning chapel due to 'neuralgia': **19**

D. Nichols (VC)

THE BRANSTON CUP FOR POETRY

Competition for the Branston Cup was strong as ever, with a record six entries for the prize. The judges would have liked to have awarded a prize to all boys who submitted their work, but finally decided by a hair's breadth that T. Beddoes's entry was a deserving winner. Congratulations also to runner-up A. de Vigny.

WINNER
The Land of Imagination

Maybe one day you will stop uttering
Relentless and ill-informed nonsense

In the sacred name of History! Look, sir,
Not a single boy is listening to a word
Nor a sentence of what you have to say.
Enough! The day will come when
Some of us you bore today will

In glory escape your influence and
Set sail for the land of Imagination in

A golden yacht for which you have
Not been

Issued a boarding pass.
Do you not think, sir, that
In the broad scheme of things your
Overview of the Battle of Marengo is a
Trifle uninspiring?

T. L. Beddoes (Lower VI)

RUNNER-UP
Food, Glorious Food

School dinners give
  me no thrill.
The morning porridge
  looks like swill.
This food goes on
  my parents' bill
But they don't believe
  I'd prefer to eat road kill
Of my own free will
If only to avoid
  the doctor's bill
When school dinners
  make me ill.

A. de Vigny (Lower IV)

STAFF LEAVING

Mr M. T. Drummond

Michael Drummond came to teach Classics at Swinesend in 1953 after serving gallantly for three years in the Korean War, from which he returned with a young wife, Kim Kang Ja, and a metal plate in his head (leading some of boys in the early 1980s to affectionately bestow on him the nickname 'Metal Mickey', after the amusing TV robot of that era).

He was a first-class scholar and Michael's teaching produced many excellent classicists. But it was on the playing fields that his heart lay. In spite of his war injuries, Michael gamely took charge of firing the starting pistol on sports day, and was always on hand to 'dry the winner' with his towel after every swimming competition.

Michael was a great wit, whose waspish comments were much in demand by colleagues and boys alike. One Old Boy recalls the time when, on his first day at Swinesend, he encountered Michael with his pipe ablaze, his gown a-flapping and his shoelaces mysteriously absent. 'Please, sir. Are you the Headmaster?' said the boy. 'No,' said Michael, quick as a flash. 'But I *ought to be*.'

Fifty-three years is a long time to serve a single school and, at Michael's age, most men would be looking forward to the peace and contentment of a well-deserved retirement. Not so Michael! We wish him good health and good fortune as he moves with his wife to Manila, where they plan to open a small boarding house for distressed young ladies.

S. T. de P. Aidre

Dr P. R. Fortescue

I first encountered Paddy Fortescue in 1985, when he was leading a party of Sixth Form scholars in a chorus of 'Kevin Barry'. Unfortunately, he overbalanced while reaching for a high note and fell backwards off the antique table on which he was standing to conduct proceedings. Typically, Paddy was able to laugh off this incident and even persuaded the landlord to write off the cost of the damage – and his tab – in return for not informing the authorities his pub had been selling alcohol to minors.

Many old Swinesians who arrived after 1980 will have their own memories of this remarkable man, whose poetic temperament and commitment to learning were exceeded only by his love of conviviality and conversation. I know that I am just one of many who are deeply grateful for being introduced to the finer things in life at one of Paddy's legendary soirées to which he invited his students to discuss their own work. Their enjoyment was enhanced by the fact that Paddy often arrived with a carrier bag full of port bottles, but without the essays, which he would eventually recall he had left somewhere on a train.

His lessons were often equally memorable, enlivened as they were by his fondness for reciting poems in Irish or Russian, even though no one in the class could understand him, and his refusal to discuss any of the A-Level set books, or even show up, before eleven o'clock in the morning. On one memorable occasion, he challenged a Sixth Former to a duel in the quadrangle after they disagreed about the role of nature in Coleridge's verse. This eagerly awaited contest was, alas, foiled by the untimely appearance of the Headmaster.

It was with great sadness that I learned that Paddy's health had obliged him to leave Swinesend. I, and many other grateful pupils, wish him well in his forthcoming transplant.

G. Darley

SWINESEND IN THE NEWS

Congratulations to G. Campbell (School) and M. Yusuf (St Leger's), who won Young Management Consultants of the Year for their plan to sack the entire teaching staff and replace them with e-learning initiatives outsourced from Bangalore.

P. Finch (Haig's) and W. Marr (School) were singled out among the young athletes competing at the English schools championships last summer by testing positive for no fewer than six hitherto undiscovered substances.

A NOTE FROM THE BURSAR
The Office of Fair Trading

Some parents have expressed concern about the Office of Fair Trading's finding that the country's leading public schools have been unlawfully collaborating in fixing their fees. Some parents have noted that Swinesend School has not been named in this connection.

We have queried this with the OFT and received the following reply: '...in publishing a list of leading public schools found to be fixing prices, the Office of Fair Trading had no intention of implying that Swinesend is not a leading public school merely because it did not include Swinesend's name in the list. Likewise, we did not wish to imply that Swinesend was not a leading public school merely because the named schools chose not to share their valuable information with Swinesend. We accept that Swinesend's fees are every bit as exorbitant as the schools named in the list and it is (therefore) a leading public school.' I hope that this answers parents' concerns.

Major T. D. Bragg (Retd), Bursar

KEEP A LOOKOUT, BOYS!

by Col. Jock Fuller-Bradlake, OS Alumnus Officer

At last May's OS Summer Party I noticed a queer-looking fellow circling around the convivial gathering. He was wearing an Old Swinesian cravat and highly polished shoes, yet there was something that made me even more uneasy. His accent. There just a hint of something foreign in it. And that car he arrived in — was it really a Triumph Stag? — it seemed far too flashy.

My curiosity aroused, I ascertained his name and immediately checked it against the OS Register. Just as I had suspected: he was an example of a most pernicious menace stalking this land. He was an Impostor! The Bursar and I despatched him quickly and cleanly.

So, when the Headmaster asked me to write for the School Magazine, my mind naturally turned to the future welfare of those of you who are leaving the School. Quite naturally, you will wish to seek out older Swinesians so that you may cultivate their friendship and patronage. But how will you know whether those chaps who are ready to beguile you with tales of the Dear Old Place, or offer you a place in their stockbroking firm, are really Old Swines at all?

At first you may see nothing wrong. Such a man may wear the finest suits. He may speak in such an accent that taxi-drivers mistake him for a nephew of Earl Waldegrave. He may be a fine sportsman or the epitome of the man-about-town; but before you submit to his blandishments, you should make sure you check the following.

The neck

The hawk-eyed boy first looks to the neck. The Impostor believes that a public school man is always to be seen wearing his old school tie. Nothing could be further from the truth. Indeed, there are very few occasions when a Swinesian wears his.

He does so when visiting an Old Swines' function, when marrying the daughter of another Old Boy — or when up to no good. It has often been remarked that an Old Swinesian tie can be a terrific help if you are into vice of any kind. The only other time when the old school tie is worn is when appearing in court for sentencing.

Verbal tics

Early in your meeting with him, the Impostor will drop into conversation the name of the School. This gives him away. The true Swinesian either knows that the listener is aware of his schooling (merely referring to his House if it is necessary) or he will be too embarrassed to refer to his education at all.

Over-familiarity

If, on first meeting, a self-styled Swinesian insists that you and he have a lot in common and ought to be close friends, you should be instantly on your guard. The only friendly approaches a Swinesian ever receives are unwelcome advances from the Chaplain. Things change little when he leaves school and, if a man addresses you by your first name, you can be sure he is a wrong 'un.

Uncommon zeal

You will, naturally, be suspicious of a man who boasts that his success in life is down to hard work, early rising and the avoidance of strong drink. The opposite is true for the real Swinesian, who prefers to get by on the strength of his wits, charm and well-placed friends.

Name-dropping

If any suspect starts to boast about the prominent people amongst his friends, your suspicion will harden into certainty. If a Swinesian refers to well-known alumni at all, it will be either in derogatory terms or in order to outline the torments he inflicted on them at school (or vice versa). If an Old Swinesian knows any powerful person educated elsewhere, he will keep it to himself (in case you want an introduction and queer his pitch).

Taste and decency

An exaggerated fondness for Gilbert and Sullivan is a sure sign of the Impostor. While one or two Swinesend men may hum the tunes with a fair degree of accuracy, none ever knows the words. What is more, you may also confidently denounce as an Impostor any man claiming to have been educated at Swinesend who has an old edition of French poetry on his bedside table.

PUZZLES FOR PREP TIME

SUDOKUSUDOKUSUDOKU

This addictive numbers game has captured the popular imagination. But this special public school version has the added advantage of being educational. It is particulary good fun when played with a friend from a more modern, or less prestigious, establishment.

The rules are the same as for the classic version – each number must appear once, and once only, in each row, column and three-by-three box. However, instead of a simple digit, the numbers used are the foundation dates of some of our most distinguished schools.

	1567		597		1440		1540	
		1611	1432		1540	1567		
1382								597
1611			1440		1584			1567
		1567				1432		
1584			1923		597			1440
1540								1382
		1584	1382		1567	1923		
	1440		1540		1611		1584	

Q.P.R. RULE!

For an added challenge, try to match the school to the dates used in the puzzle. (For answers, see foot of page)

Dates:
597, 1382, 1432, 1440, 1540, 1567, 1584, 1611, 1923

List of schools *(in alphabetical order)*:

Charterhouse
Eton College
King's School, Canterbury
Rugby
Sevenoaks
Stowe
Swinesend
Uppingham
Winchester College

OLD SWINESEND NEWS

The OS Lodge

The OS Lodge held its annual meeting shortly after Easter in the crypt
beneath the Masonic Hall. A number of important people attended.
OS's wishing to join the lodge are requested to visit the duck pond in
Hyde Park on October 3, next year. The code word is 'Swinesend'.

OS Dinners

This year's London dinner was held in the Highland Steakhouse,
Charing Cross Road. Guest of Honour Sir G. Cleveland (Cockchafer's
56) spoke about his fascinating business in the eastern European
recruitment industry. The Moldovan
waitresses he provided for the occasion
were a great addition to the
festivities!

The East Midlands dinner was
held at the Glasgow Rangers
Supporters Club, Corby. Guest of
honour, Msgr Cecil Crosbie (St
Leger's 65) was sadly indisposed
following a vigorous theological

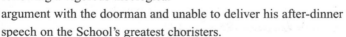

argument with the doorman and unable to deliver his after-dinner
speech on the School's greatest choristers.

Last September, members of Cockchafer's from 1965–80 were reunited
at the funeral of their former Housemaster, J. C. Burgess. At the
reception, held in the Ufford Arms, many former pupils toasted his fond
memory with champagne and an impromptu firework display until 6 a.m.,
when the police requested that they put a stop to the reminiscences –
which had kept many of the townsfolk awake!

This year's most exotic OS event was the Shanghai Dinner held in the
Hall of the Eternal Proletarian Revolution (sponsored by Coca-Cola). The

Headmaster, as guest of honour, was presented with a most gratifying cheque in recognition of the number of OS's who have been employed in a consultancy role with the Chinese State Prison Service in recent years.

Valete

It is with great sadness that we announce the deaths of the following OS's, listed in order of the date they left school. May they rest in peace.

1901 BAILDON, Cedric Cecil (Haig's). Suddenly in a chainsaw accident in the Amazon rainforest. Cedric was the oldest living Swinesian but, at 123, was still enjoying an active and fulfilling life in charge of his own logging business. Married late in life, he is survived by his wife, Lola (28), and their three children.

1920 YULE, Frederick Percy (Fellsgarth). Caught in crossfire on Hackney's Upper Clapton Road. Frederick ran a very successful furniture business in the area and was renowned for his trademark carved chair legs.

1933 DANZIGER, Marcus Robert (School). Drowned in a vat of Malmsey whilst tending to his cellars in the south of France.

1934 ROBERTSON, Cyril Stokes (Cockchafer's). Eaten by a spotted hyena whilst charting the badgers of Lower Bantustan.

1940 WASHBURN, Francis John, the Right Reverend (St Leger's). Expired whilst bringing his mission in person to the house of Madame Eve in his diocese of Soho and Chelsea.

1954 MOORE, George Robert (Fellsgarth). Died mysteriously in San Juan prison, Guatemala, where he was awaiting trial on a charge of importing arms with the intention of overthrowing a neighbouring government.

1964 IPPY, Rupert Stone (School).
Psychedelically and rapidly
after attempting to fly
unaided from the roof of
Ely Cathedral.

1999 MACDONALD, Ranald Gregor Campbell (St Leger's).
Suddenly of an obesity-related heart-attack.

2000 STOREY, Rebecca (Keppels). Run over by an Israeli Defence
Force bulldozer in the West Bank. Rebecca's youthful idealism ended,
inevitably, in tragedy whilst she helped the Israelis demolish the homes
of suspected terrorists.

2001 IBRAHIM, Mohammed Tariq (School). Tragically killed in a
plane crash in the United States.

2005 WHITE, Jeremy Jason (Cockchafer's). Peacefully from ennui
in his room at St Andrews University, moments after coming to the
conclusion that everything worth doing had been done before.

the eNd

THE OLD SY
ASSOC

ODI PROFANUM VULGUS ET ARCEO

FREE ACCESS TO W

'INESIANS'
ATION

BENEFITS OF MEMBERSHIP INCLUDE:

- FREE USE OF THE SWINESEND CLUB HOUSE

- FREE CUT-OUT-AND-KEEP OLD SCHOOL TIE

- FREE SCHOOL PHOTOGRAPH (IN THE STYLE OF MESSRS GILLMAN AND SOANE OF OXFORD)

- FREE INTRODUCTION TO THE OLD SWINES' OWN MASONIC LODGE

- CUT-PRICE MEMBERSHIP OF THE SWINESEND SCHOOL LEISURE CENTRE

- RIGHT TO JOIN NUMEROUS AFFILIATED CLUBS including the OS Cricket Club, Rugby Club, Soccer Club, Snooker Club, and the OS LGBT Collective.

W.SWINESEND.COM

FEEL INA

Failed to get int

No sporting achieveme

If so, don't worry:
there is a solution at hand.

AS A MEMBER OF THE OS
ASSOCIATION YOU CAN
IMPRESS YOUR COLLEAGUES,
CLIENTS OR PUPILS
WITH YOUR VERY OWN FREE OLD
SCHOOL PHOTOGRAPH TO HANG
ON YOUR OFFICE WALL

DEQUATE?

a School Team?

s about which to brag?

SWINESEND SNOOKER TEAM: MICHAELMAS [*insert date here*]
Back row (l-r) R.W.F. Tish-Groper; A.R. Seboil; B.A. Bishop-Soper; S.T.D. Ladyman; B.O. Pitts.
Front row (l-r) L.S. de R. von G. St J. Smith; M.C.C. Bibbling-Clipe; [Insert your name here];
N.O.I. Woggle-Puller; P.N. Ringscratcher; C.L. ap Waites.